IDEAS FOR GREAT

75¢

KIDS' RO

DESIGN: JEANESE ROWELL INTERIORS

*A Western ranch was the inspiration for this theme room featuring
rough-hewn pine bunk beds, a leather easy chair, a rustic clothes pole,
Indian-design pillows, and outdoor gear including a lasso and fishing creel.*

DESIGN: JUVENILE LIFESTYLES, INC.

The pulls and other geometric cutouts adorning the bed, dresser, and corner cabinet were hand-painted to harmonize with the bedding and curtains.

Book Editor
Lynne Gilberg

Research & Text
Susan Lang

Coordinating Editor
Kathryn Lescroart Detzer

Design
Joe di Chiarro

Illustrations
Susan Jaekel

Editor: Elizabeth L. Hogan

First printing October 1993

Photographers: Peter Aaron/Esto, 25 bottom, 63; **Amisco Industries, Inc.,** 74 right; **Lea Babcock,** 65 bottom; **Laurie Black,** 68 bottom, 89; **Andrew Bordwin,** 13, 14 top, 22, 25 right, 27 bottom, 28 top, 38 top, 40, 44 top, 52 top left, 53 bottom, 57 bottom, 69 bottom right, 84 right, 93 bottom; **Child Craft,** 18 middle left and bottom left, 43 bottom right; **Cosco,** 78 top left; **Crandall & Crandall,** 52 top, 53 top, 58 top; **Stephen Cridland,** 60 bottom, 62 top, 74 left; **Mark Darley/Esto,** 54 bottom; **Design Horizons by Ladd Furniture, Inc.,** 79 top; **eurodesign, Ltd.,** 15, 54 top, 76 bottom, 77 middle; **Richard Fish,** 43 left; **Fisher-Price,** 84 left; **Scott Frances/Esto,** 9 top, 10, 35, 64 top; **Fun Furniture,** 49 bottom, 85 bottom; **Michael Garland,** 9 bottom, 24 bottom, 30 left, 56 bottom, 59, 87; **Shelley Gazin,** 91 top; **Jeff Goldberg/Esto,** 21; **Philip Harvey,** 1, 2, 4, 5 bottom, 6, 8, 20, 23 bottom, 24 top, 32, 33, 36, 38 bottom, 39, 41, 42, 44 bottom, 45, 48, 51, 52 bottom, 53 top left, 56 top, 64 bottom, 65 top, 66, 68 top, 69, top, 70, 72, 73 top, 78 bottom left and right, 79 bottom, 81, 82, 86, 88, 90, 92, 94, 96; **Lands' End,** 5 top, 77 top; **Stephen Marley,** 46 top; **Norman McGrath,** 23 top; **Norman A. Plate,** 93 top; **Kenneth Rice,** 77 bottom; **Southern Living Magazine,** 14 bottom, 29, 43 top right, 67 left, 69 bottom left; **Techline by Marshall Erdman & Associates, Inc.,** 27 middle, 46 bottom; **3M,** 31; **Brian Vanden Brink,** 47 top, 61; **Vander-Schuit Studio,** 18 top, 28 bottom, 30 right, 58 bottom, 60 top, 62 bottom, 67 right, 73 bottom, 76 top, 50; **John Vaughan,** 91 bottom; **Visador Company,** 83; **Darrow M. Watt,** 27 top; **Whitney Brothers,** 85 top; **Doug Wilson,** 49 top; **Tom Wyatt,** 57 top.

Go to your room...

What a pleasant banishment if the room is as inviting as the ones shown in this book! The following pages are packed with wonderful ideas for planning, decorating, and shopping for kids' quarters—plus plenty of photographs of real rooms and new products to review for inspiration.

We thank the following for providing props for some of the photographs: Azrock Industries, Inc.; BetLar Products, Inc.; Calico Corners; California Kids; Circus Floors; Citation Carpet Mills; eurodesign, Ltd.; Hold Everything; Imperial Wallcoverings; Jonathan Kaye; Juvenile Lifestyles, Inc.; Kids Furniture and Lullaby Lane; Lakeshore Learning Materials; Marin Designer Showcase; National Floor Products Co.; Palacek; Rubbermaid; Samson-McCann; San Francisco Decorator Showcase; Wallpapers to Go; and Wroolie and LoPresti.

We would also like to thank Dr. Oscar L. Frick of the University of California at San Francisco and George Krall of the Colgate Mattress Company for sharing their expertise with us and the Fox Elementary School in Belmont, California for sharing their students' ideas.

Special thanks go to Marcia Morrill Williamson for carefully editing the manuscript and to JoAnn Masaoka Van Atta for styling some of the photographs.

Cover: Built-ins along one wall provide ample storage space and a cozy place to curl up with a good storybook. A pretty floral design repeated in the bedding, wallpaper, and window treatment gives the room a coordinated look. Cover design by Naganuma Design & Direction. Fabric Treatment by Muffy Hook. Photo styling by JoAnn Masaoka Van Atta. Photography by Philip Harvey.

CONTENTS

SPECIAL FEATURES

FOCUSING ON KIDS

In the past, a child's room tended to be treated like any other bedroom in the house. The room was outfitted with standard furniture, and frequently bore the same color scheme as the rest of the home. Only the belongings revealed that the occupant was not an adult.

Sometimes stereotypes took over the decor, resulting in frilly pink furnishings in a girl's room and what were generally regarded as "masculine" colors and accessories in a boy's.

Now there's a growing recognition that a child's room should be designed to suit one particular child, and that the space is not only a place to sleep but also a personal environment that needs to fulfill many roles—play area, study hall, hobby center, meeting site, and storage locker.

It's not enough just to create a functional, comfortable room. Kids today are more style conscious than ever, about everything from running shoes to pillow covers. They want their rooms to look cool. That means getting the right colors, the right furniture, and the right accessories.

(Even if your child isn't yet old enough to have strong opinions about room decor, it's only a matter of time

Harlequin-motif puppet theater occupies a corner play area. The young puppeteer can hang belongings on the whimsical clothes pole.

DESIGN: CROWORKS AND JOYCE BOHLMAN DESIGNS

before individual preference and peer pressure kick in.)

Although you'd like to please your child, you certainly don't want a room so trendy that you have to overhaul it repeatedly to keep pace with changing fads. This book shows you how to create a room with long-lasting appeal that's also open to adaptation.

In the following pages, you'll find all the nuts-and-bolts information necessary to devise a workable plan. For inspiration, thumb through the gallery of photographs. Then turn to the shopping guide for product information and buying tips.

Coordinating bedding, window treatment, and wallpaper border establish a nautical theme.

A cozy sleigh bed and a building-shaped cupboard are prominent features in this blue and white room. Checks and plaids tie together the decor and convey a homey feeling.

A PLANNING PRIMER

Adults use many rooms of the house, but kids pack most of their living into a single room. A bedroom may be a sleeping chamber to a grownup, but to a kid it's also a place to listen to music, play games, sprawl on the floor, roughhouse, read, study, build models, daydream, visit with friends, and stash innumerable possessions. That's asking a lot from four walls!

You'll need to plan carefully to create a room that serves all those functions, yet is comfortable and inviting—and has enough staying power so you don't have to redecorate every few years. This chapter guides you through the process, starting with some general observations about children's needs and seeing you through to a specific plan for your own child.

Bright colors create a cheery atmosphere for the occupant of this compact but well-organized space. The low sleeping loft, accessible by scarlet ladder rungs, contains plenty of storage below. A desk extends from one side.

7

DECORATING CONSIDERATIONS

In the case of any room, including your child's, the physical layout—not only the dimensions but also the locations of windows, doors, electrical outlets, telephone jacks, and heating vents—dictates many decorating decisions. Of these "givens," electrical outlets and telephone jacks are usually the easiest and least expensive to change, so don't feel boxed in if they are inconveniently placed.

Budget is another important constraint. If there are no limitations, you can do whatever you like—buy a roomful of coordinated furniture or hire a designer to create a fantasy-satisfying refuge. Otherwise, you'll have to prioritize your needs. You may want to invest most substantially in a few good pieces, such as a solidly constructed bed and dresser, and spend less on the rest of the furnishings. Or you may want to buy modular pieces that can be added to or reconfigured over the years.

You don't have to buy everything new. There's a large market for used furnishings for kids. Just make sure that any secondhand items you acquire are safe and sturdy.

Beyond physical and budgetary limitations are other considerations more directly related to your child. A nicely decorated room may look great to

WINDOW TREATMENTS & ACCESSORIES: DOENDA SMITH

This pretty room was designed for a young girl who likes feminine things. Remove the dolls and stuffed animals, and the decor is sophisticated enough to take the resident into her teen years.

parents and friends, but unless the style and contents suit the child, he or she won't fully enjoy the room. Here are some observations to help you start defining your own child's requirements.

Age

Obviously, the arrangement should be appropriate for your child's age. A toddler feels comfortable in a room with a low bed, small-scaled chairs, pictures of nursery-rhyme characters, lots of stuffed animals, and brightly colored accessories—whereas a budding teenager would be mortified to bring friends home to such a room. Kids develop so quickly that you have to be on your toes to keep up with their evolving needs and tastes; see pages 13-15 for basic room requirements at various ages.

You'll also have to consider the desired life span of the decor. If you intend to redecorate frequently, you can indulge in furnishings that appeal to a limited age group and change the look when it's obvious that your child has outgrown it. But if you want the decor to last longer, more planning is required. You'll have to think ahead if you want the same basic furnishings to serve your child from infancy to young adulthood, with only slight modifications over the years. Many parents take a middle road, opting to redecorate every six or seven years.

Personality & Interests

Like adults, children feel more at home in rooms that reflect their personalities and interests. There is no generic kid's room, just as there is no standard room that will appeal to all adults. If you're fixing up a nursery, the decor will reflect your own preferences. But it doesn't take much time for youngsters to exhibit traits and tastes that can be expressed in the decorating process. If they're old enough, include them in the planning; such involvement may also motivate them to take better care of their things.

Rather than build the decor around a specific person with specific likes and dislikes, you may be tempted to let gender guide you. But be aware that your child might not be happy with the results. Your young daughter may love a room filled with pink ruffles—or she may prefer a play loft that allows her to jump and climb. Don't count on your young son relishing a sports theme just because he's a boy. He may be more interested in astronomy.

DESIGN: SARA OLESKER, LTD.

A child's zeal for computer games suggested a room's decor (top)—easily altered with a change of bedding and window treatments. These young girls (at right) enjoy furniture their own size.

Planned Activities

Since kids really *live* in their rooms, allow space for the many activities that will take place there: playing, studying, reading, pet care, painting, listening to music, and entertaining friends. If there's a separate playroom, some of these activities can be accommodated there.

Unless there's a permanent place elsewhere in the house for your child to build model ships or conduct science experiments, plan a hobby area in the bedroom even if it's a tight squeeze. That way, you won't have to keep clearing the kitchen table or living-room floor, and your child's efforts won't be repeatedly disrupted.

Scale

Homes are designed and furnished for the comfort and convenience of adults. At least in their own rooms, kids should have a sense of control over their environment. They should be able to hang up clothes, reach toys or books, sit in chairs their own size, and look at pictures without having to crane their necks.

Placement of furnishings is important from the start, since children discover much of the world by touch. Toy shelves, drawers, and pictures should be placed low in baby years. "Out of sight, out of

DESIGN: SUNDAY HENDRICKSON

mind," so keep possessions visible and within easy reach of little kids. Also, if children can't reach their belongings, they have to rely on adults to get what they need—or they may endanger themselves by trying to climb up and grab what they want.

When planning a room for a young child, think small—imagine that you've shrunk to less than half your height. The real challenge is to arrange the room so that it stays in scale with a youngster who grows bigger each year. Adjustable furniture—shelves that can be rearranged or a table with a top that can be raised—is a wise investment.

Red, yellow, and green combine in a fresh way in this room. The color scheme is all the more striking set against beige walls and carpeting.

Furnishings should also be in scale with the surrounding space. It's jarring to have a tall canopy bed in a tiny room with a low ceiling, or a diminutive dresser in a cavernous room. Having a lot of large furniture in close quarters can overwhelm a child, just as too-sparse decor can engender a sense of loneliness.

Colors

You might prefer a fairly neutral palette in the rest of the house, but no such inhibitions apply in a kid's room. Here, anything goes—including bold, brassy colors and wild combinations. In fact, a committed color scheme helps you choose coordinated furnishings. You can use color to set a mood, unify disparate elements in the room, or define territory in shared quarters. Color can even have a coding function, helping children know where to return playthings, books, or clothes after use.

The color wheel, at right, provides some basic information. Among the pure hues, the most powerful are the primaries—yellow, blue, and red, the

source of all other colors. Secondary colors (green, orange, and violet, formed by combining primary colors) are a little weaker, although still vivid. Intermediate colors, created by mixing a primary with an adjacent secondary color, have less impact.

Most kids love bright, unadulterated colors until they're about 10. Avoid an all-white, sterile-looking room, since young children need visual stimulus. Also refrain from using a lot of very dark or deep colors for fear of creating a dreary or oppressive atmosphere. Extended colors—those to which a little black, white, or gray have been added—are a great choice for teens, since they produce a more sophisticated look than pure colors do.

There are two schools of thought about choosing colors for kids' rooms. Some experts advocate letting even toddlers pick their own colors, on the theory that they will be drawn to ones that fulfill some psychological need. Others advise parents to make the aesthetic decisions until the child develops a good sense of color preference, which can happen as early as age three or four. Even when youngsters can't verbally express their feelings

Color Wheel

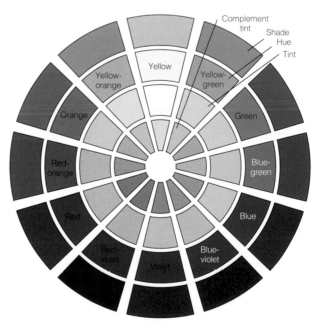

The color wheel locates primary colors (yellow, blue, and red) at equidistant intervals around a circle; transitional colors connect them. Each pure hue is labeled. Adding black to a color makes a "shade"; adding white makes a "tint." A "complement tint" is formed by adding a bit of the color opposite on the wheel.

SAFETY TIPS

A safe environment is important at all stages of life, but it's critical for young kids. Here are some simple measures to make your child's room safe.

Cribs & Beds

■ Make sure the crib conforms to current safety standards; see page 73. For tips on buying cradles and bassinets, see page 72.

■ Keep an infant's bed free of long ribbons, cords, and hanging toys that the baby might reach. Remove crib gyms and mobiles when the baby is able to push up onto hands and knees.

■ When your child leaves the crib for a bed, attach a low guardrail if the sleeping surface is more than a foot off the floor. Placing the bed in a corner, fenced by walls on two sides, adds a measure of safety.

■ Reserve the top level of a bunk bed and other elevated beds for kids at least six years of age.

Electrical & Heating

■ Keep lamp and appliance cords out of reach so the baby can't tug or chew on them.

■ As soon as your baby begins to crawl, cover unused outlets with safety caps and replace broken or missing receptacle cover plates.

■ Use a wire reel to keep excess lamp cord neatly stored.

■ Eliminate extension cords whenever possible by rearranging furniture. If you must use an extension cord, unplug it when not in use.

■ Screen off any unguarded heating register, radiator, or other heat source.

Windows

■ Keep crib and playpen far enough from windows so your child can't yank on curtains, break glass, or climb out the window.

■ Don't put climbable objects under windows.

■ Install window locks that allow only partial opening so a small child can't fall out.

■ Keep drapery, shade, and blind cords out of reach of young children. Shortened cords and wands are available by special order. If you don't want to cut a long cord, wrap it around a cleat mounted high on the wall.

Furnishings & Storage

■ Use a changing table or mat with raised sides and a safety strap.

■ Arrange furniture to make sure your child won't climb to dangerous heights.

■ Store toys and games low to the ground, and keep potentially dangerous items such as lotions or scissors high and out of reach.

■ Make sure a lidded toy chest has safety hinges to prevent the lid from slamming shut. Safer choices for toy storage include open chests, plastic bins, and low shelves.

■ Position storage hooks either above or below your child's eye level.

■ Get sturdy, well-constructed furniture, since you can't predict how a child will use it. Look for smooth or rounded edges, not sharp ones.

■ Anchor tall or unstable furniture to the wall.

Miscellaneous

■ Get rid of small objects that could find their way into a crawling baby's mouth. Also avoid decorating a toddler's room with accessories small enough to be swallowed.

■ Keep baby care products well beyond a tot's reach. Use a diaper pail with a childproof lid.

■ Use throw rugs with skidproof backing.

■ Install smoke detectors to comply with local codes.

■ Make sure that walls, furniture, and toys are free of lead-based or other toxic finishes. This might be a danger with any surface painted before 1978, when regulations outlawing lead in paint went into effect. If you find lead (special swabs for detecting it are available), remove it while wearing an approved breathing device, eye protection, and old clothing that you can throw away; don't sand the finish, or you'll fill the air with lead dust. Apply a new, nontoxic finish specified for children's products.

■ For the latest information on warnings and recalls on children's products, call the Consumer Product Safety Commission hotline at (800) 638-2772.

about color, they often provide clues—for example, in the colors of crayons or construction paper they most frequently choose. Some kids favor toys of certain colors.

If you consider your child's taste extreme, limit the preferred color to wall paint—it's far easier to repaint than to replace all the furnishings. Or highlight that color in the bedding, which you will probably need to replace in a few years anyway.

Maintenance

A child's living space isn't a showroom—it's a place where a real kid spends a lot of time working and playing as well as sleeping. Filling the room with fragile, easily marred furnishings or ones that absorb dirt and stains is asking for trouble.

Even generally tidy kids aren't saints (and neither are their friends), so don't expect too much of them. Not only do accidents happen, but also kids can be expected to let loose from time to time. Choose materials that make it easy to maintain the room, no matter who's in charge of tidying up—you or the child.

The younger or more careless your child, the more durable and easy to clean the materials should be. Look for hard-wearing, spillproof, dirt-resistant surfaces for the floor, walls, and furniture. Good choices include scrubbable vinyl wallpaper, wood with a waterproof finish, and laminate tabletops. And washable fabrics are more practical than those that must be dry cleaned.

Noise Control

Controlling noise may be an important factor, depending on the type of activities taking place in your child's room and the room's location relative to other living areas in the house. The sound of incessant music or boisterous play may drive you crazy if your child's quarters are near a room where you or other family members spend a lot of time.

If your house is large, consider moving the noisemaker to a more remote part of it. But if you're stuck with the current setup, choose materials that deaden sound. Cover the floor with wall-to-wall carpeting or a large area rug, and use cork or another bulletin-board surface on the walls and ceiling.

DEALING WITH ALLERGIES

You can take steps to minimize your child's suffering from allergies without going to the extreme of stripping the room so bare that it looks like a monk's cell.

Reducing the amount of dust in the bedroom, since that's where your child spends so much time, will improve the problem dramatically. A significant allergen is the house dust mite, a microscopic creature that lives in house dust and feeds on natural fibers and on skin and dandruff shed by humans. The mites are prevalent in bedding, natural-fiber carpeting, and cotton-linters (the stuffing in mattresses and upholstered furniture).

Cut down on exposure to mites by encasing the mattress and box spring in dustproof plastic protectors that zip shut; get the kind sold by companies specializing in allergy products (allergists usually provide order forms). Some plastic mattress cases sold through mass merchandisers tend to sweat and crinkle.

When furnishing the room, avoid upholstered furniture and choose synthetic materials rather than natural fibers. Instead of feather-filled pillows, use polyester-filled ones. Cotton sheets and blankets are all right, as long as they're washed frequently. Choose washable rather than dry-cleanable window treatments. Stuffed animals should also be washable.

Hardwood or resilient floors are preferable, but if you must have wall-to-wall carpeting in your child's room, make sure it's made of nylon or another synthetic material and not wool. Throw rugs that can be laundered frequently are fine.

Avoid dust catchers. Anything that isn't moved regularly, such as the contents of a bookcase, accumulates dust. Keep surfaces as clear as possible so they can be dusted or vacuumed two or three times a week.

Filters will prevent forced-air heating systems from spreading dust through the house. You can get filtering units for individual vents or a single filter for the whole furnace.

Ban any pets with hair, fur, or feathers from your child's room. You don't have to deprive a pet lover, though—cold-blooded animals, such as fish and turtles, won't cause any harm.

AGES & STAGES

A room that suits your child perfectly at one stage of development can be pretty hard to live with at another. Kids change so much in such a short time that you need to be alert.

The following are basic requirements for different age groups. They're generalizations that may or may not apply to a particular child, but they can give you a rough idea of what to expect. If your child doesn't fit the mold, forget about generalities and pay attention to what he or she is telling you verbally or through behavior cues.

Infancy

An infant needs only a safe place to sleep and to be changed. Plan to provide convenient storage for diapers, toiletries, and clothing and a comfortable chair where you can feed and cuddle the baby. You'll also want to have an overhead light on a dimmer, a nightlight, and a window covering that allows the room to be darkened. Once you take care of these basics, you can decorate the room however you please—but realize that you're doing it more for yourself than baby.

Newborns can't see well enough to appreciate a nursery decked out in frills or peopled with storybook characters. Even though their eyesight gradually improves (by the age of six months, they can focus on details across the room), babies appear happiest with a limited amount of stimulation.

Babies are interested in sights and sounds close to them. Until they're about six to nine months old, they see black and white and other sharply contrasting colors the best. Simple patterns seem to elicit the most pleasurable response—for example, three dots representing the eyes and mouth of a human face, a bull's eye, or a checkerboard.

An infant's senses of touch and hearing are almost up to adult standards. Babies like a variety of textures and soft, melodic sounds. They're more interested in tactile objects and in crib toys that move or play music than they are in a static wallpaper pattern or furniture with a juvenile theme.

Once a child starts to crawl and then to walk, safety becomes even more vital; for measures to protect tots, see page 11. Even though toddlers have senses that are more finely developed, they still aren't old enough to appreciate nursery decoration.

If you want to keep things simple, you can satisfy your baby's requirements and yet create a room pleasing to the adult eye. The style of the furniture along with the color of the crib bumpers and bedding can give the room personality. You might like to round out the decor with details such as a wallpaper border or a shelf of stuffed animals.

Two to Five

This is a time of great exploration, as youngsters climb on furniture, take things apart, and poke into everything they can reach. Keeping safety in mind, stock the room with sturdy, spillproof furnishings and keep breakables out of reach. Walls should be washable and floors hard-wearing and easy to clean.

Children appreciate decoration now, especially images of favorite storybook or cartoon characters, and they love bright colors. A chalkboard, bulletin board, artist's easel, or continuous roll of paper will provide a safe outlet for creative urges.

Your toddler can go directly from the crib to an adult-size bed, or you can opt for a smaller bed that will last until about age five. Some kids will kick up a fuss about an intermediate bed, demanding a standard-size one like the other kids have.

At this stage, youngsters need lots of toy storage. Keep it low so they can reach items and put them away easily. A toy chest or several color-coordinated bins can handle this job. Toys could also go on low shelves or in drawers under the bed.

DESIGN: LEWIS OF LONDON

Infants seem to appreciate simple black-and-white patterns within close view, such as the designs on this crib mobile and bedding.

DESIGN: LITTLE ONE'S HAND PAINTED FURNITURE

Propped in a corner, a fancifully painted folding screen with door and window cutouts creates an enchanting hideaway for two- to five-year-olds.

Ample play space is also important. Younger kids like to play wherever parents are, so toys usually end up all over the house. Older kids are more comfortable playing in their rooms by themselves. The floor is the favored place for play, so you'll want to keep a good portion cleared. If the room has a wood or resilient floor, add cozy throw rugs or an area rug to create soft places to sit.

A child-size table and chair set provides snug seating for crafts, painting, puzzles, and tea parties. The tabletop should be large enough for art projects and the chair should be low enough so your child's feet rest on the floor. The more comfortable the child, the longer he or she will stick to the task.

Other essential items are a bedside table and lamp. Choose a window covering that can dim the room if you want your child to sleep when it's light outside. Young kids don't usually have many articles of clothing that need hanging, so a dresser, stackable drawers, or a wardrobe with plenty of shelf space is usually sufficient.

Six to Eight

At this stage, kids are developing strong opinions about decor and can participate more in choosing furnishings or rearranging the room. Listen to your young ones and take them shopping with you, but be prepared to help them compromise, since their choices may not be sufficiently practical.

Despite how grown-up they may seem at times, they're still kids. Even though they attend school full time, they also spend many hours in their rooms and so need plenty of play space. Your child is now old enough for a high platform or climbing structure, if you want to incorporate one.

Kids this age are mature enough for elevated sleeping, in a loft bed or the top level of a bunk bed. This is about the time they begin to ask for sleepovers, so think about providing a trundle bed or some other guest accommodation.

It's time to replace child-size tables and chairs with larger furniture that can be used for homework. Add lighting to illuminate study, reading, and other specialized task areas in the room.

The need for storage only seems to grow as kids get older. To make room, you may want to stow seldom-used toys and games elsewhere in the house or give them away. Modular storage units will allow you to add capacity as your child needs it.

DESIGN: KATHERINE WALDEN. DECORATIVE PAINTING: AUDREY P. RABY

Six- to eight-year-olds need plenty of places to stash toys and ample floor space for play. The decor here is playful, but not too juvenile.

The well-organized study area in this preteen's room incorporates a pop-up dressing table. The wreath over the bed provides another grown-up touch.

Nine to Twelve

Decor assumes new importance at this stage, and many kids like to take charge of fixing up their rooms. Give them a good surface for tacking up posters and other doodads if you want to preserve the walls.

Although kids in this age group still play, they now engage more seriously in sports and hobbies. They begin collecting things in earnest—rocks, baseball cards, books, animal figurines, whatever strikes their fancy.

As they approach the teenage years, youngsters become increasingly intolerant of anything that seems babyish. They no longer want to be associated with a climbing or other play structure or items with a juvenile theme. They may ask for more grown-up belongings—for example, your daughter may want a dressing table with a mirror.

Storage is a major consideration, since kids need room for collections, games, books, and assorted possessions. Now is also when they begin needing space for more—and longer—clothes.

Youngsters have more homework now and need good study areas. Your child may be ready for a computer in the room. If you've been holding off on purchasing good carpeting and window treatments, your child may now be responsible enough to justify installing them.

Teens

At this stage, kids become increasingly independent. They spend more time away from home and when at home, especially in their own rooms, privacy is paramount. A teen feels that his or her room is a personal domain, to be run without interference.

Relics of early childhood are an embarrassment. Your teen may even consider bunk beds too childish, so you may want to unstack them to use as twin beds. Other easy ways to give the room teen appeal are to swap old bedding and window treatments for more sophisticated ones, and to trade small throw rugs for a larger area rug. Toning down bright primary colors on the walls and ceiling can also make the room seem more grown-up.

There's more homework now than ever before, so your teen needs a good study space with plenty of room to spread out books. Another requirement is an area for listening to music. Seating for friends is also a must—it can be in the form of a day bed, folding chairs, or floor pillows.

A teenager wants to be able to accommodate a growing wardrobe. Storage areas previously used for toys can now house hobby materials, collections, books, sports gear, a stereo system, and electronics equipment. Since your teen's reach has increased, you can install higher shelving.

Teenager's room features sophisticated accessories and a modular wall system that stores study and hobby gear.

PARTNERS IN PLANNING

The ultimate experts on what kids like best are kids themselves. It makes sense to bring your child into the planning process since he or she has to live in the room. Helping to plan the room and pick out items for it also instills a feeling of self-worth and pride.

Don't expect young kids to understand the concept of room coordination. They may want furnishings with colors and patterns that clash wildly. You may have to inject some order into the process—but don't modify your child's concept so much that you deal it a deathblow.

Don't expect every desire expressed to be realistic—not many parents have the budget or space to install a swimming pool or jacuzzi in a kid's room. But keep an open mind. Some of the ideas may be workable just as they are, others may need a little refinement, and still others may spark more practical inspirations.

For fun, we asked a group of fifth graders in Belmont, California, to describe their dream rooms. Here is a sampling of their responses in words and pictures.

After I watch my big-screen TV, I can relax and read a good book. In my reading nook there are a lot of soft pillows and warm blankets. There is also a big green beanbag chair that squishes when I sit on it.

—Allison

My dream room has a gorgeous canopy bed and closets full from shopping. My bed has a peach comforter and satin pillows of every color. The high canopy has pink flowers and pretty peach drapes that I can close at night.

—Meghan

My dream room has a secret area in the wall where you can hide money, a diary, or anything else personal. You open it by pushing on one side of my green-and-black bed.

—*Jason*

Wouldn't it be fun to have a computer with all sorts of games and a window that can change its scenery just by pressing a button?

—*Mina*

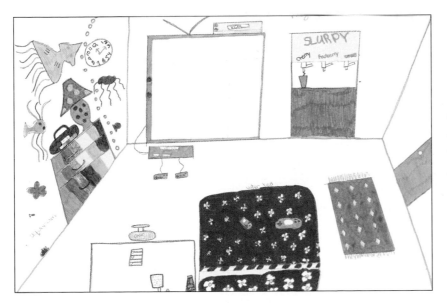

My dream room has a beautiful aquarium and a refreshing slurpy machine. The aquarium serves as my wall and has many tropical and unknown fish in it.

—*Renee*

ROOM TO GROW

You can rightly expect a newly decorated living room or master bedroom to stay pretty much unchanged for many years. But a kid's room shouldn't be static. You can't fix up a room for a young child and think your decorating chores are finished until your offspring leaves for college.

You can choose to redo the room completely every time your youngster outgrows or tires of the decor—but that's unnecessary, not to mention expensive. If you plan well and decorate with an eye toward the future, you'll be able to modify the room periodically to meet the needs and tastes of a developing child.

The key is to build flexibility into the decor. One of the best ways to do that is with adaptable furnishings—pieces that can be added onto, reconfigured, raised, or converted to another purpose as your child grows.

Here, the crib can be moved out and an adult bed slipped in without rearranging all the furniture. The crown molding will create a canopy effect over the bed.

This crib converts from sleeping quarters for a baby to an intermediate bed for an active young boy or girl. Just detach the side rails, add a mattress extender, and move the chest of drawers to the side.

Modular Furnishings

Many manufacturers offer modular room groupings that include beds, dressers, work surfaces, bookcases, and other components. The modules can be configured to your child's requirements and then rearranged as needed. Make sure that what you choose now will be usable later on. Bookcases may hold stuffed animals today, but they should be suitable for school texts or encyclopedia volumes tomorrow.

A modular closet system is also practical over the long haul. The shelves, drawers, poles, and other components can be rearranged as your child grows.

Although often considered part of a closet system, sturdy stacking drawers and bins can have other uses. For example, drawers can be stacked to create a low dresser for a small child. When your child outgrows the dresser, restack the drawers to support a plywood or laminated desktop. Stacking bins make wonderful storage containers: start low and stack higher as your child gets taller.

Convertible Furnishings

Convertible furniture offers flexibility. Many kids' stores sell dressers with a top that serves as a changing table, then later flips over to become a toy or knickknack shelf. You can also buy cribs that convert into day beds and toddler beds, or toddler beds that convert into adult-size beds. A sturdy cart that you use for baby supplies can support a television set or a stereo system later on.

Infancy

Ages 6-8

Ages 2-5

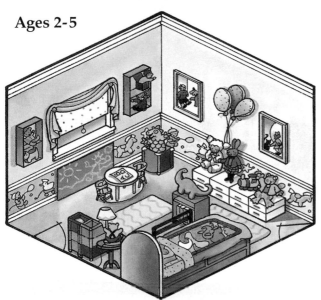

Ages 9-12

Teens

If planned well, a child's room can serve admirably from infancy to young adulthood with relatively few changes over the years. Stacking drawers, a rolling cart, and wall-hung shelves are constants in this room. The drawers start out as a storage unit and base for a portable baby changer, then restack at different stages into a low dresser, a low desk, and, finally, a standard-height desk.

At appropriate stages, the cart holds baby supplies, toys, a radio, and then a computer. The shelves house stuffed animals during the early years, schoolbooks later on. Periodically switching to more sophisticated styles of bedding, lamps, pictures, and window treatment ensures that the room keeps pace with the child's development.

Most bunk beds are versatile. Some accommodate either a mattress or a desktop insert in the lower bunk. Many types unstack to become twin beds—a wonderful feature if your offspring decides that the bunks he or she craved a few years ago are now too juvenile.

Adjustable Furnishings

Pieces that can be raised or lowered are also practical. A secretarial chair gives years of use, since the height and back support are adjustable. One manufacturer makes a table and bench set that adjusts to three different heights for toddlers to preteens. Various mechanisms for adjusting furniture can be built into custom pieces. For example, a desktop might slide into a series of notches or slots at different heights so the work surface can be raised as the child grows.

In the same way, position pictures and other wall decorations low when your child is young, then move them up. Wallpaper borders, moldings, and storage hooks are other wall items that little children appreciate placed low but older kids prefer higher up.

DESIGN: SETTERLUND INTERIORS

An irregularly shaped room partition, covered in an abstract wallpaper pattern to match the window shade fabric, provides young siblings with privacy. A personalized wallpaper border placed diagonally over the beds identifies each child's territory. A consistent use of red, white, blue, and yellow throughout the room helps unify the separate spaces, as do the identical bedding and the repetition of the pencil-motif border above the window.

ROOM FOR TWO OR MORE

Planning a room that will be shared by brothers or sisters is much more challenging than arranging one for a sole occupant. That's because the shared room must meet the needs of each resident for space, individuality, and privacy. The ideas offered below will help you make the best of togetherness.

Even if the room has only one regular occupant, you'll be wise to plan for overnight guests. That way, you won't throw the room into a shambles every time you try to put up a visitor.

Sharing with a Sibling

Sharing a room has a positive side—companionship—but it also has a negative aspect—lack of privacy. With two or more kids in close quarters, it's inevitable that they'll get on each other's nerves now and then. However, if you plan well, you can create a room that keeps its residents happy most of the time.

Remember that a shared room must accommodate kids with different personalities and interests. Forsake the idea of a theme room or other highly specific decor unless both kids fancy the concept. A less precisely defined decor, such as one based on a color scheme or built around a modular furniture grouping, will give the kids more freedom to express their individuality.

Because roommates are forced to spend so much time together, it's important to give each child personal space. Assign the kids their own drawers and closet space, and provide each with a place for hobby equipment and displays. The children should also have their own desks or study areas, preferably apart from each other.

Separate play areas are important if the kids are far enough apart in age to need different toys and games. Individual areas will discourage the younger sibling from grabbing the older one's possessions and deter the older sibling from carelessly stepping all over the younger one's belongings.

The bed often serves as a private retreat in a shared room, so arrange the sleeping quarters to maximize privacy. Bunk beds are a good choice, since the kids can't see each other when they're in bed. Other solutions include arranging twin beds on each side of a painted plywood panel or placing the beds at right angles with a table between them.

Physical dividers (like the plywood panel) are a clear way to define territory and provide privacy.

Many other kinds of dividers can be used: a two-sided shelving unit or bookcase, a wallboard partition that goes partway up, a row of stacking storage units, a folding screen, or curtains hung from the ceiling.

Sometimes psychological divisions are just as effective as physical ones in marking territory. For example, color coding each child's area makes it perfectly clear who has the rightful claim on what furnishings.

If you want to keep squabbles to a minimum, be fair when allocating space. Try to divide it so that each occupant has access to desirable features, such as windows and closets.

It's easier to design a room with the possibility of a second child in mind than to try to cram in an extra bed after the fact. You can always use a spare bed for a visiting child, even when the room has only one real occupant.

Making Room for Friends

Children enjoy sleepovers, so plan a place for young visitors to sleep. No one will get any rest if the kids are piled into one bed without room to stretch out.

You may want to get bunk beds for a single child so the extra bunk can accommodate a guest. A trundle under your child's bed is another good solu-

DESIGN: JAMES STEWART POLSHEK & PARTNERS

An extra bed serves as a comfortable couch for one or extra seating for friends during the day and at-the-ready sleeping quarters for an overnight guest.

DESIGN: McMILLEN, INC.

DESIGN: NOEL JEFFREY

In both rooms above, the sleeping area is well defined without being the most prominent feature. In the top photo, a valance and curtains hung from crown molding produce a canopy effect that is light and airy, even though the bed is placed in a corner against two walls. In the bottom photo, the bed is nestled in a corner alcove away from other room elements.

tion. So is either a day bed or a futon, either of which can also serve as a comfortable lounging place. If the room is large enough, you might want to put in twin beds.

A child-size couch that converts into a guest bed is suitable for little kids. Stow-away options that can work for children of all ages include sleeping bags, air mattresses, and folding cots.

ROOM ELEMENTS

Besides providing sleep and play areas, accommodating hobbies and collections, and storing belongings, the room should be a pleasant place for your child to live. Achieving this will be easier if you break the room into its separate functions and figure out how you want to handle each one.

The following section discusses the room elements generally; for more information about furnishings, see the shopping guide on pages 71-95.

Sleeping Space

When planning the sleep area, start with the obvious: don't block doors, windows, or heating vents. Avoid putting a young child's bed under a window—but if there's no other option, install a lock so the window can't open wide enough for the child to fall out. A more secure location is a corner of the room, where two sides of the bed will be protected. (For more about safety considerations, see page 11.)

For the first few months of life, your baby can sleep in a bassinet, cradle, crib, or even a padded drawer or basket. A crib is the best choice from about three months to when the youngster begins to climb out regularly or attains a height of 35 inches. At that point, the child can move to an intermediate bed, suitable until about age five, or take the big step to an adult-size bed. If you're worried about the child rolling out, you can start by using the mattress alone on the floor, without a frame.

Generally, manufacturers recommend that top bunks and loft beds remain off-limits to kids under six. But you'll have to judge the abilities of your own child. Some six-year-olds aren't ready for high living, while some younger kids are adept at scampering up and down ladders and can be trusted in an elevated environment.

Your child's preference is important, but other factors enter into the choice of a bed, such as its cost, how long you want it to last, and how much space it requires. And some beds may suit your decorating scheme better than others: a wooden four-poster bed will seem more at home in an old-fashioned room, while one with a tubular metal frame will look better in a contemporary scheme.

If saving floor space is important, think about such options as loft beds, wall beds, and trundles. A loft bed gives your child more than just a place to sleep—it incorporates storage and study or play

Each youngster has his own toy storage and display space in a shared room (top), where carpet and bare floor provide surfaces for different types of play. A corner play area (bottom) features a child-size sofa and chair, plus a coffee table with a painted-on chalkboard surface.

areas. A chest bed or captain's bed, with its built-in drawers, is a good choice for a small room with limited storage space. Many other bed designs offer the option of under-bed drawers.

Perhaps your child craves a fantasy bed, but your budget won't allow it or you don't want to invest in a piece of furniture that will last only a few years. With a little imagination, you can satisfy both your needs and your child's. Transform an ordinary bed by attaching a plywood headboard cut in the shape of a castle, tree, animal, or other object. Paint the headboard or cover it with fabric. When the child outgrows the illusion, unbolt the headboard and replace it with something more conventional.

Play Areas

Most of the floor space in a young child's room should be allocated for play. Although little kids will sit at a low table, they really like to sprawl out on the floor with toys and games. Some playthings require a smooth, level surface, while others are fine on carpet-

ing. You can plan for a hard surface through most of the room, with a few throw rugs to provide comfortable places to sit or lie.

In a small room, maximize floor space by arranging the furnishings against the walls. A bed that folds up or slides away is a great space saver. One that has built-in compartments or under-bed drawers provides lots of storage room without taking up extra floor space.

Kids love cozy nooks. If your child doesn't need all the available closet space for storage, you could turn the closet into a hideaway or puppet theater. If the closet is large enough, you may be able to build a loft—anchor a sheet of sturdy plywood to the inside closet wall at any height and affix a ladder to the loft surface. Cover the plywood with a thin foam mattress and pile it with pillows. To create a simple theater, remove the closet door and put up a curtain with a cutout area for puppets. Remember, you'll need lighting inside the closet if it's to serve as a play area.

If you buy bunk beds for one child, the extra bunk can be used as a play area when it's not serving an overnight visitor. Attach curtains to the sides to create a private retreat or secret clubhouse. (Bunks are often sold with optional curtains or tents.)

Study Areas

A well-designed study area will foster good study habits and neatness. Your child will be better organized and more likely to consult reference books if bookshelves are within easy reach above or to the side of the desk. Handy shelves and drawers will also encourage your youngster to keep the desk clear. If supplies must be hauled back and forth from across the room, they'll tend to stay piled on the desk.

A little table or desk will do as a homework area for a kid just starting school, but a well-organized study area becomes important later. The basic requirements are a work surface (at least 2 feet deep and 4 feet wide), a comfortable chair, and good lighting. Computer equipment requires extra space. If the study area is to double as a craft or hobby center, you'll need to make sure the work surface is extra-large.

A modular study center allows you to add components, including extra work surface, as needed. If you opt for a loft or bunk unit that incorporates a desk, be sure the desk is big enough to serve your child throughout school. Having to add more work surface later defeats the purpose of buying such a space-saving structure.

Some children are easily distracted if the study area is in front of a window or if the desk chair can swivel. You have to know your child when you plan the study setup.

Hobby Areas

If your child has a hobby that can be conducted in the room, then plan a place for it. For example, a plant lover could use deep windowsills for container gardening. An astronomy buff could set up a telescope in front of a window that offers a good view of the night

A child-size table and chair set, like this one made of molded plastic (top), is an ideal place for a tot to do puzzles and artwork. Compact study center (bottom) features a drafting table, a filing cabinet, a bulletin board, and shelving.

sky. For an avid reader, a comfortable armchair in a well-lighted corner near a bookcase is heaven.

Combining the hobby and study areas is fine if it's easy to stash away schoolbooks and hobby gear between uses. For some hobbies, such as sewing, it's much more convenient to leave equipment out until a project is finished. In such cases, you'll want to plan a separate hobby area if the room is large enough.

If your child wants to keep fish, hamsters, mice, or some other creatures in the room, you'll need to plan an area for them. Allow enough space so that the aquarium or cage isn't in danger of being knocked over, but is still accessible for easy cleaning. You'll also have to take the animals' needs into account—for example, whether they should be kept away from heating vents or direct sunlight.

Furniture

You have many options when shopping for a child's room. Your choices will depend largely on your budget and on how much flexibility you want. You can order from stock or have a piece custom-built. Ready-

ARCHITECT: LES WALKER

A youngster with many interests stocks his hobby area with a microscope, tools, and paints. Shelves are specially designed to store specific items.

These prettily painted pieces are part of a furniture collection. Later, the changer top can be removed and a coordinating bed can substitute for the crib.

made furniture can be stand-alone, modular, or part of a furniture collection; custom pieces are often built-in. To stretch a budget, you can buy unfinished pieces or tap the large market of used furniture. The pros and cons of the various options are discussed below.

No matter what kind of furniture you choose, make sure it is sturdy and has no sharp or protruding edges. Easy-to-maintain surfaces are important—for example, sealed wood, laminates, or metal. For tips on shopping for furniture, see page 80.

Stand-alone. This furniture is movable: you can rearrange it, shunt it into another room if your child no longer needs it, or take it with you when you move. But unless the piece is custom-made, it comes in standard dimensions—so you may not be able to get the exact size and configuration you want.

Modular. Modular furniture offers great flexibility, allowing you to combine components—such as a bed, headboard, shelves, drawers, cabinets, and work surfaces—to fit your child's exact needs. Many of the units stack or abut to form larger composites. You can add components (if the manufacturer still makes the item when you're ready to buy) and reconfigure the whole arrangement as needed in the future. The components can be packed up when you move and rearranged in a new room. Some modular systems require assembly.

Furniture Collections. Many manufacturers offer collections of furniture—often as many as a few dozen pieces that coordinate in style and finish. A collection designed for a kid's room may include several different choices among stylistically coordinated beds, headboards, bedside tables, dressers, armoires, bookcases, hutches, desks, chairs, and framed mirrors.

Built-in. Ready-made furniture that fits an area precisely can sometimes give a built-in look, but more often such pieces are custom-made. You can build furniture into nooks or under windows, creating a seamless look and utilizing space that might otherwise be wasted. A custom built-in can be expensive, and you can't usually take it with you when you move.

Unfinished. Well-constructed unfinished furniture is usually a good value. Pieces made from soft white pine are the least expensive—and also the least durable. Sturdy pieces made of knotty pine, maple, or birch are a step up in quality and price. The best-quality and costliest items are usually made of solid oak or cherry. You can customize unfinished furniture with hardware and a painted, stained, or clear finish.

Used. You can often get a good deal on used furniture, but pay close attention to safety. Make sure the piece is sturdy and well made. A secondhand crib should conform to current safety standards (see page 73). Be wary of old paint, which may contain lead; for information on removing a suspect finish, see page 11.

A ROOM FIT TO LIVE IN

Children enjoy their rooms more when they can sit comfortably at the table or desk, and when many of their possessions are at eye level or within easy reach. This chart containing average measurements will help you create a safe, livable environment for your child.

AGE	HEIGHT	EYE LEVEL	HIGH REACH	TABLE HEIGHT	CHAIR HEIGHT
3	37	33	41	15	8
5	39-47	35-43	43-52	18	10
7	44-52	40-48	49-59	19	11
9	47-57	43-53	53-65	21	12
12	53-64	49-60	61-73	23	13
15	61-71	57-66	70-82	26	15
Adult women	61-70	57-66	70-81	29	18
Adult men	65-75	61-70	74-86	29	18

Measurements are in inches.

Ideal Shelving Dimensions

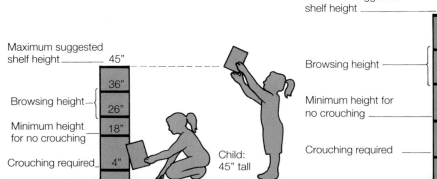

Regularly used items should be placed at less than maximum reach so kids can get them without straining or standing on tiptoes. Put often-used objects on higher shelves when kids grow taller.

Storage

Adults usually want to keep items that aren't in constant use hidden in cabinets or behind closed doors, but that's not always the best kind of storage for kids' rooms.

The idea is to organize the clutter so that the room looks neat, yet the child knows where to find things. It's perfectly fine to keep articles in sight, but arranged on open shelves or stuffed into boxes, bins, and other receptacles. Clear, covered containers are a good solution if you want to keep possessions free of dust.

Even clothes can be kept in plain sight. Removing a closet door for a year or two reminds youngsters who are learning to dress themselves that they can enter the closet and select an outfit for the day. Remember, little kids can hang up their own clothes only if the pole or hooks are placed low enough for them to reach.

Storage needs change over the years. At first, you'll need containers for diapers and baby supplies. Then your young child will need places to stow toys and games, stuffed animals, art materials, storybooks, and clothes. Next, space will be required for schoolwork, hobbies, collections, electronic equipment, and sports gear. The same units you start out with can continue to serve your growing child—if you plan carefully and don't lock yourself into juvenile themes.

If the room is small, look for units that use space efficiently. Under-bed drawers provide handy storage—and indulge a child's love for throwing things under the bed. Other space savers include storage units that stack on the floor, attach to the wall, or hang from hooks. A built-in storage area, such as a window seat with storage inside, utilizes space well, although you can't take it with you when you move.

Many types of bins and boxes are sold expressly for storage, but you can press into service any number of other containers, some of them found around the house. The myriad possibilities include shoe boxes, empty coffee cans (check for sharp edges), plastic jars, cutlery trays, and fishing tackle

Tower of tubs (top) makes order out of chaos and is fun to climb. Modular wall unit (middle) contains lots of storage room and even a clothes hamper. Shelf unit (bottom) stores larger items at the base and smaller items higher up.

DESIGN: TECHLINE BY MARSHALL ERDMAN & ASSOC., INC.

DESIGN: MOTIF DESIGNS

boxes. Color coding or using symbols on the containers will help your child remember what goes where. Don't forget a "lost-and-found bin" for unidentified odds and ends.

If you want to promote neatness, locate storage near the activity area. This may not be where you think your child should be conducting the activity, but be realistic. Art supplies should be stored near where your child draws or paints. Toys should be stored near where your child tends to play.

Flooring

The flooring in a youngster's room does more than just provide passage from one point to another. Children spend much of their time on the floor, at first crawling and then playing and drawing. Even older kids often read or listen to music while lounging on the floor. So the floor should be comfortable, safe for play, and easy to maintain.

You can choose a smooth, level surface (wood or a resilient flooring such as vinyl), a soft surface (wall-to-wall carpeting or rugs), or a combination.

For a very young child—from crawler to early school years—the best floors are smooth surfaces with some give. Both resilient and wood floors cushion falls, clean up easily, and can be kept dust-free. They also provide a nice flat surface for stacking blocks and rolling balls.

Wall-to-wall carpeting is usually recommended for older kids, since it's harder to keep clean and doesn't work well for toys that need a perfectly level surface. But a low-pile industrial-grade or indoor/outdoor carpet is an inexpensive option that stands up to little kids and is fairly flat.

A combination of hard and soft surfaces can be very successful. For example, a vinyl floor has a smooth, level surface for a toy train set, while fluffy throw rugs provide cozy areas for reading a book or watching television.

The flooring can even be a source of fun and learning. Several manufacturers make area rugs and wall-to-wall carpeting with boards for checkers, chess, and other games printed on the surface—they sell the game pieces, too. You can also get rugs and carpeting with learning motifs, such as how to tell time or read the alphabet. Of course, you can paint the same sort of designs on a bare floor or on a large piece of canvas that can be unrolled for play and then stowed away.

Young girl's room features built-in cabinets for storage and display. The flat-woven, decorative dhurrie rug makes a cozy play surface.

Walls & Ceiling

The walls and ceiling in a child's room offer great decorating potential, more so than in other rooms of the house. That's because kids' rooms invite a playful, sky's-the-limit approach.

A little paint will transform the room. You can keep it simple—solid colors on the walls and ceiling,

The fabric braiding on the walls echoes the rug border and cabinet molding. The ceiling features shirred fabric with a center rosette.

SPACE SAVERS

Coping with skimpy space is a common problem in today's small-scale bedrooms. Here are some ways to maximize your child's territory.

■ A loft bed makes optimum use of floor space because so many functions are served within the footprint of the bed. The sleeping area is on top, with storage and a play or study area beneath.

■ Stacking bunk beds take up the space of a single bed, yet accommodate two kids. If there's only one child, the extra bunk serves as both play space and guest accommodation.

■ A disappearing bed, such as a wall bed, clears the decks for play or hobbies.

■ Under-bed drawers, offered as accessories for many types of beds, utilize what would otherwise be wasted space. Bins, boxes, and other portable storage units that fit underneath the bed are just as useful.

■ Hooks, shoe bags, and pouches hung on chair-rail molding or on the backs of closet or room doors provide off-the-floor storage.

■ A hinged work surface or table folds against the wall when not in use, liberating floor space for other activities.

■ Shelving units that hang on the wall instead of sitting on the floor free up floor space.

■ An organized closet with shelves, stacking baskets, and other modules holds much more than a standard one.

■ A minimum of furniture makes the room seem more spacious. Look for multipurpose pieces, such as a toy box with a bench top or a bed with built-in storage.

and a contrasting trim. If you want something more creative but don't want to hire a professional, here are some simple ideas: paint clouds or stencil stars onto the ceiling, brush a rainbow onto the wall, or let your child help you spatterpaint the walls with bright colors. Another simple technique: buy sponges in the shape of fish, letters, numbers, or other objects (or cut them out yourself if you can't find the design you want), dip them into paint, and print the walls or ceiling with them. If you opt for a professional, then you can choose from many decorative techniques, including murals and trompe l'oeil.

Wallpaper offers additional options. You can use a single pattern or coordinate two or more—and cover all the walls or just one. You can even cover the ceiling with such patterns as a starry sky or fluttering birds. Be just as creative with wallpaper borders: circle the ceiling, ring the walls at your child's eye level, or outline the windows and doorway.

Although paneling may seem more appropriate for a den or study, it can be used imaginatively in a kid's room. For a casual look, choose a light wood or paintable finish, and install the paneling only partway up the wall; add a decorative wood molding and coat with a protective sealer.

Other practical wall treatments include chalkboards and bulletin boards. Create an art area by applying special chalkboard paint on a section of wall—it can be a plain rectangle or a whimsical shape, such as the silhouette of a whale or a boat. You can wall-mount a store-bought bulletin board or create your own pinup surface by covering a wall with cork or fabric-wrapped fiberboard.

DESIGN: KATHERINE WALDEN. DECORATIVE PAINTNG: AUDREY P. RABY

A balloon valance made of plywood partially covers a towering window, bringing it down a little and making it less intimidating to a small child.

A mural of a fox den (at left) camouflages the entrance to a storage area. Recessed lights over the headboard and in the ceiling slope augment natural light in a teen's bedroom (above). Table lamps provide additional illumination.

DESIGN: LAUREN ELIA. DECORATIVE PAINTING: PATRICK SHEEHEE

You can give walls additional interest with pictures, posters, wall hangings, moldings, and decorative shelves. Some manufacturers sell decorating kits in various motifs. Designed to be used by children, the kits come with repositionable borders and appliqués. Keep track of your child's growth by attaching a decorative tape measure to the wall.

You can buy glow-in-the-dark ceiling appliqués in the shape of stars. Suspending objects, such as model airplanes or kites, is another great way to decorate the ceiling. If you're handy with a sewing machine, make some plump, white pillows in amorphous shapes; hung from the ceiling, they'll look like clouds.

Windows & Doors

Since kids spend many daylight hours in their rooms, choose a window treatment that lets in plenty of natural light. The treatment should also be capable of dimming the room if you want your child to sleep when the sun's shining.

Options include curtains, blinds, shades, and shutters. If you're buying for the long term, choose a treatment that's durable, easy-care, and no trouble for your child to operate.

The color or pattern of the window treatment can provide much of the visual appeal. Some companies offer ready-made curtains and shades to match bedding, or you can sew them yourself from sheets. You'll also find coordinating fabrics available with many wallpaper patterns. Shutters will take on

new life when painted a lively color. Plain shades or curtains can be customized with fabric paints or glue-on designs.

Other ways to decorate a window include outlining it with a wallpaper border, stenciling a design around it, dangling a mobile in front of it, or building a window seat underneath it.

Don't forget the door when you're decorating a kid's room. You might outline it with paint or wallpaper, paint your child's name on it in decorative stencil-on letters, or incorporate it into a wall mural. You can put the back of the door to practical use by building a storage unit on it or turning it into a bulletin board. Delight a young child by removing the closet door and replacing it with a curtain for a puppet theater or a secret clubhouse.

Lighting

There's more to illuminating a child's room than just choosing decorative fixtures. You must also consider function and safety.

Designers divide lighting into three categories: ambient, task, and accent. The first two are the most important in kids' rooms. Ambient lighting provides a soft level of general light, while task lighting focuses stronger light on an area where a visual activity, such as reading or homework, takes place. Primarily decorative, accent lighting is less commonly found in a child's room, although you might decide to install some to highlight a trophy case or doll collection.

Babies are most comfortable with soft, diffused light from an overhead fixture on a dimmer or a table lamp with a low-wattage bulb. The soft glow from a night-light will reassure the baby, as well as guide you into the room late at night. Parents may want to have a stronger light available near the changing area.

Ceiling fixtures are the safest type of lighting for very young kids, since they're out of reach. They provide general illumination needed for play and make the room less scary. Also plan on having a table lamp within easy reach of your child's bed.

As your child grows, add task lighting for art projects and puzzles and later for homework and other activities requiring concentrated light. A task light shouldn't cast a shadow or create glare. Too much contrast between the illuminated area and the adjacent area can strain eyes. Experts recommend keeping the surrounding area at least a third as bright as the lighted area.

Task lighting should be positioned at the proper height for your child, so that the work area is illuminated but the child isn't able to see the light bulb when seated next to the fixture. Lighting for a computer should come from overhead; if it comes from the side or from behind, it creates glare on the screen.

If an opaque shade doesn't provide enough light, replace it with a translucent shade, which will diffuse light to a larger area. You can also install dimmers to control the amount of light.

For specifics about the types of lighting fixtures and bulbs or tubes appropriate for kids' rooms, see pages 94-95.

TYPES & STYLES

There's no need to choose a particular style or type of room when you decorate. The room can be eclectic, or it can be a one-of-a-kind creation that defies pigeonholing. But in case you do opt for a specific type of room, here's some information about a few of the most common ones.

Theme Rooms

Living in a room that looks just like a scene from the Old West, a jungle, the deep sea, or the interior of a spaceship may appeal to your child—but think carefully before you decide to implement such a theme.

Some child specialists argue against theme rooms that are so realistic they resemble movie sets, so detailed they leave nothing to the imagination. These experts recommend treatments that give kids the chance to exercise their own imaginations.

For a circus theme, for example, there's no need to set up three rings with a life-size figure of a ringmaster, a bed in the shape of an elephant, and a mural of acrobats and performing animals. Instead, you could find thematic bedding and a wallpaper border. Complete the fantasy with three-dimensional fabric balloons on the walls, a tentlike canopy over the bed, and rows of stuffed animals that your child can orchestrate in pretend performances. You've gotten across the feeling of a circus without cramping your child's creativity.

Another reason not to invest too much time and money in creating a truly authentic-looking scene is that kids' interests are apt to change rapidly. Recognizing that, restrict the theme to items that can easily be replaced, such as a comforter, curtains, posters, a wallpaper border, or a headboard that can be unbolted.

A theme based on a child's serious, long-standing interest or hobby—such as ballet, astronomy, football, or horseback riding—is likelier to stay the

DESIGN: 3M

A decorating kit offers a fast, simple way to create a theme room. Available in many thematic designs, the kits contain borders and precut appliqués that can be moved around repeatedly without damaging the walls.

The delicate frills and flourishes in this room evoke a romantic period in history, without being true in every detail to a particular era.

course than a standard theme picked at random. As your child learns or achieves more in the chosen field, he or she can augment the decor with newly acquired paraphernalia or with ribbons or trophies.

Period Rooms

The use of certain colors, details, and materials will help you create a room reminiscent of a particular historical period, such as Early American or Victorian.

Early American is a simple, unpretentious style. Its hallmarks are quilts, rag rugs, plain curtains, crude wooden toys, and simple stencil decorations on the walls, floors, and furniture—the latter usually made of pine, maple, cherry, or hickory. Low-post beds and trundles were typical of the period. And the colors most often used by the colonists were off-white and earthy shades of brown, green, and blue.

If the Early American style celebrated simplicity, Victorian decor reveled in ornateness. The telltale signs are overstuffed furniture, rich dark colors, busy patterns, layered window treatments, cornices, wainscoting, and a profusion of knickknacks. The wallpaper designs and room ornaments often related to discoveries of the period, such as automobiles and steam trains, and it was common to combine several patterns. Mahogany was a popular furniture material, as were wicker and rattan.

A room needn't be faithful to its style in every aspect. For example, if traditional Victoriana seems too oppressive for a child, feel free to lighten the colors, simplify the window treatments, and avoid some of the clutter. For an Early American motif, there's nothing wrong with introducing a modern quilt pattern or colors the colonists didn't use.

Contemporary Rooms

Another option is a room with clean lines and sleek, modern furniture. Don't worry about the room being too sterile or stark for a youngster. Visual appeal can come from the color scheme or from the decoration.

Such a room often displays artifacts of pop culture—for example, it might boast neon lights, posters of celebrities, logos of trendy companies, or high-tech images.

The decor can easily become dated if it relies too heavily on current culture. To avoid that problem, limit the number of images so that they can be easily replaced, or use only classic ones.

Several materials are suitable for furniture in a contemporary room: wood, tubular metal, plastic, glass (but avoid the latter in a young child's room). Laminates also work extremely well.

PUTTING IT ALL TOGETHER

Where do you start? A good beginning is your child, if he or she is old enough to voice decorating preferences. (For a sample of what happens when you ask for opinions, see pages 16-17.) Your offspring may have definite ideas for the room—and, if you're lucky, these may be easy to implement. If not, they may suggest other, more workable notions that appeal just as strongly to your youngster. If the gap between your taste and your child's is wide, you may have to reconcile some differences before proceeding.

One of the attractions of a theme room is that it offers clear direction: once you have the theme, you just look for elements that fit it. For example, you would choose such items as a captain's bed, a sea chest, cargo netting, and wooden crates for a nautical theme. A period room offers just as plain a path: you look for furnishings that recall the chosen era in history.

This contemporary room, with its flamboyant and flashy mural, exhibits the energy and vitality of its young sports-loving occupant. Rollerblading and skateboarding are among favored activities.

DISPLAYING COLLECTIONS

Kids love collecting objects—including ones that have no intrinsic value but are important to them. They're proud of these items and enjoy looking at them and showing them off to friends.

The type of collection will often suggest the method of display. Objects that sit on a flat surface—for instance, rocks, dolls, stuffed animals, and albums—can be arranged on shelves. Some collections can be affixed to the wall—an assortment of hats hung from hooks screwed into picture molding, or autographed pictures of sports celebrities on a bulletin-board surface. Prize ribbons for sporting events can be arranged in acrylic plastic frames and hung on the wall. Model airplanes can be suspended from the ceiling. Small, round, or colorful objects like marbles can be stored in transparent containers on a dresser or bookcase.

You may want to install a glass-fronted cabinet to show off an attractive collection and keep it dust-free. Wait until your child is old enough to treat breakables with respect. A young child is better off with open shelving—it's safer, and the displayed objects are more accessible.

A visually appealing collection may merit accent lighting. Place directional lights above the collection and focus them on the objects.

Pulling together the decor for other types of rooms may not be as obvious. One tactic is to start with a centerpiece—for example, an appealing wallpaper pattern, colorful bedding, or a special piece of furniture, such as a loft bed or an antique wardrobe—and build the decor around it. Then coordinate other furnishings with the central item.

Another approach is to start with a color scheme. If you and your child decide on a green, yellow, and white room, look for furnishings that fit the color scheme—and pretty soon the room will take shape.

Unfortunately, ideas don't always spring forth full blown and complete in every detail, so you may be looking for help. This book is designed to spark ideas. Other good sources of inspiration include friends' houses, kids' stores, furniture showrooms, catalogs that sell children's products, decorating magazines, fabric shops, and wallpaper stores.

If you see a concept you like, you don't have to use it intact. You can borrow parts of it, or reinter-

Plan Drawings

If you were designing a room for a nine-year-old boy who needed a place for an aquarium, a cozy reading nook, a study area, and lots of storage, you might come up with one of these basic plans.

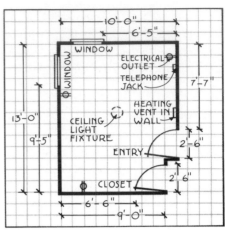

FLOOR PLAN

PLAN A

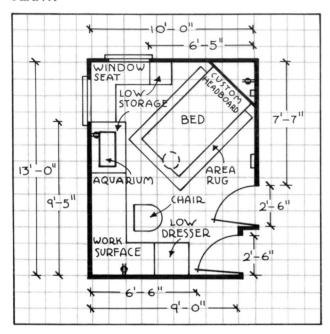

PLAN A ELEVATION

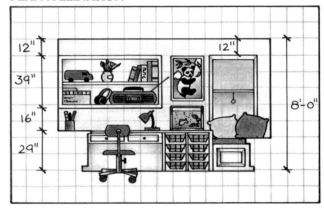

Plan A features a built-in window seat, modular furniture, and wall-hung bookshelves.

PLAN B

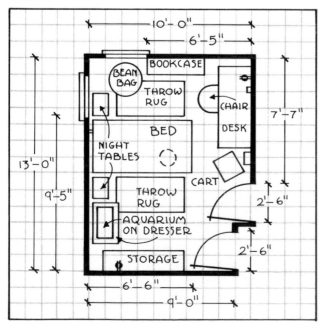

PLAN B ELEVATION

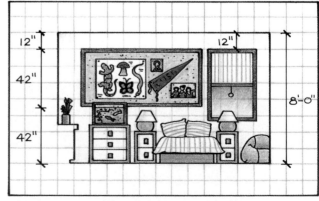

Plan B provides a beanbag for the reading nook and uses stand-alone furniture.

pret it. If you decide to replicate a room, remember that real rooms rarely look as picture-perfect as ones in magazines and showrooms. To avoid disappointment, try to envisage the room occupied by your child and a clutch of belongings.

Resolving Differences

What if you just can't go along with your child's wishes for the room? Your youngster may want to plaster the whole room with images of a popular cartoon or movie character whose appeal may take a nosedive the next year. Or the desire may be for a luminous purple and orange room, when the rest of the house is decorated in neutral tones.

You'll have to judge the depth of your child's yearning and whether vetoing the expressed preference outright will cause problems. Compromise may be in order. If your child won't be happy without the cartoon character, you could limit the image to posters or pieces of memorabilia that don't dominate the room and can be easily replaced when the attraction fades.

In the case of a color scheme that you find offensive, you could swallow your revulsion and use the colors your child likes. But you could tone them down just enough so that they become more acceptable to you without losing their magic for your child. You could also restrict the colors to wall paint so that the scheme could be easily changed in the future.

Planning on Paper

Before becoming committed to a particular decor or actually purchasing any furniture, experiment with your ideas on paper to be sure they will work. If the furnishings you want to use don't fit the space well, you may have to rethink your design. And if you're short on ideas, the process of mapping out the room may inspire you.

Measure the room, including the closet, then draw it to scale on graph paper. With the appropriate program, you could lay out the room on a computer. Either way, be sure to mark the windows and doors, and draw an arc to show which way the doors and any casement windows swing. Indicate all electrical outlets, light switches, permanent lighting fixtures, telephone jacks, and heating vents. Show all the dimensions on the plan.

Next, you can start on the room design. If you're working manually, develop your ideas on photocopies or on tracing paper laid over the graph paper. If you're using a computer, save the original, and work on a copy of the file.

Unless you plan to change the locations of outlets, switches, jacks, or vents, work around them as you place furniture. Also be sure to leave enough room to open doors fully, pull back chairs, extend drawers, and make the bed.

Having lots of open floor space doesn't matter in an adult's bedroom, but it's critical in a young child's. Leave as much floor area clear as possible for playing and spreading out toys.

Function should win over aesthetics when the two clash. Your child should be able to travel directly from one key area to another. Clothes are more likely to be hung up if your child can move easily from the bed to the closet, and toys are more apt to be put away after use if toy storage is convenient to the play area. A well-planned room doesn't guarantee neatness, but does encourage it.

Drawing a floor plan will help you see how everything fits, but don't stop there. Elevation drawings, which show the furnishings against the walls, can give you an even better idea of how the room will look. If you like, use marking pens or crayons to approximate the color scheme.

DESIGN: SARA OLESKER, LTD.

Clear passage from one functional area to another was designed into this room.

DESIGN: CYNTHIA BRIAN OF STARSTYLE INTERIORS

GREAT KIDS' ROOMS

Need ideas to get your creative juices flowing? The following pages are filled with innovative ways to treat whole rooms as well as individual room elements, such as sleeping nooks and storage areas.

As you thumb through the gallery, notice novel ways to allocate space and to use colors and furnishings. There are ideas for saving space and for sharing it, as well as ways to bring fantasies to life and fashion kid-pleasing hideaways. Pay particular attention to all the little touches that turn an ordinary space into a special one.

Treatments range from whimsical to worldly, and from old-fashioned to sleekly modern. There are even rooms cool enough to merit a kid's stamp of approval.

Camping under the stars (and stripes) is an everyday adventure when the bed is a mattress with a tent canopy. Three different wallpaper patterns are cleverly combined to carry through the patriotic theme, established by flags and red, white, and blue bedding. A bright red ceiling fan keeps things cool during hot weather.

37

FOR BABIES ONLY

DECORATIVE PAINTING: ANN BLAIR DAVISON

DESIGN: CARYL HALL STUDIOS

The charming flower-filled wall mural will be cherished for many years after baby outgrows the white-enameled iron, four-poster crib. The most detailed sections of the garden were positioned at a young child's eye level.

This whimsical scene of clowns and other circus favorites can be moved or stowed away when baby outgrows it. That's because the characters were painted on canvas rather than directly on the wall.

If baby gets bored while being changed, she can admire snapshots of herself arranged in a humorous montage. The fanciful, hand-painted changing table holds nursery supplies on an open shelf and in a cabinet camouflaged by a scene of a fruit orchard.

This fun-filled, multifunctional loft unit (above) contains a rooftop bed, an entertainment center built into the stairway, fenced-in toy storage under the window box, and a playhouse at the back (at right). A birthday party is in progress in the playhouse, which features a spacious built-in couch and desk.

SPACE SAVERS

This one-of-a-kind bench is more than just a comfortable place to lounge and read—the cutouts turn the base into a dollhouse. In later years, the recesses can hold other decorative items.

DESIGN: CROWORKS AND JOYCE BOHLMAN DESIGNS

*A junior farmhand will love this droll decor paying homage to the colorful
holstein. The barn serves double duty as a headboard and storage chest complete
with cabinets and drawers.*

DESIGN: JUVENILE LIFESTYLES, INC.

DESIGN: KATHERINE WALDEN. DECORATIVE PAINTING: AUDREY P. RABY

Panels slide to reveal storage space beneath the built-in window seat. The seat cushion is covered in a pretty yellow and blue fabric complementing the hand-painted design on the panels.

DESIGN: ARLENE ORLANSKY OF DANIELS INTERIORS

This overlapping bunk unit has a built-in desk and two bookcases— one over the desk and the other in the interior wall accessible to the occupant of the lower bunk. Folding steps take up less room than a ladder.

This bedroom grouping fits a lot of features into a little space. A drafting table with multiple tilt positions easily handles homework. Hutches border the chest bed, which slides in slightly to couch depth. A wardrobe at the foot of the bed provides additional storage.

DESIGN: LITTLE ONE'S HAND PAINTED FURNITURE

A symmetrical arrangement keeps peace between sisters sharing a pink, floral-motif bedroom. The morning-glory design on the headboards and bedside table is hand-painted.

Bunk pillars and a panel beneath the tabletop define each child's space at a two-sided desk. Two rolling drawers, one for each resident, are tucked away under the lower bunk.

DESIGN: JUVENILE LIFESTYLES, INC.

SHARED SPACE

DESIGN: JUVENILE LIFESTYLES, INC.

*Sisters share a spacious storage unit concealed by a clubhouse facade.
A combination bench and toy box, decorated with a flowerpot, pulls out from
the unit. Cutouts in the doors, one for each child, serve as puppet theaters.*

SHARED

SPACE

DESIGN: JAN TETZLAFF/ARABESQUE

A wall unit acts as a room divider, creating two spaces that seem like separate rooms. They're furnished quite differently to suit the dissimilar ages of the two residents.

There's room for two regular occupants in the bunks, plus an overnight guest in the trundle. The twin desks are set at either end of the bunks for maximum privacy.

DESIGN: TECHLINE BY MARSHALL ERDMAN & ASSOCIATES, INC.

SHOW & TELL

The type of collection determines the best method of display. A colorful grouping of buoys hangs from the ceiling in the room at right. Below, bookcases hold a bevy of dolls and stuffed animals.

A young fan displays sports memorabilia atop a cabinet and on the wall. Several peg racks hold caps from favorite teams. Punctuating the theme is a wallpaper border displaying sports graphics.

A model train chugs along on a track set on a high shelf circling the room. Background scenery was cut from plywood, painted, and screwed to the wall. Trees cut from medium density fiberboard were painted and glued in place in front of the track.

DESIGN: FUN FURNITURE

Side-by-side cases contain open shelves for books and knickknacks, plus tiny glass-fronted cabinets to protect delicate figurines. A hand-painted floral design decorates the cabinet doors and top molding.

THEMES & FANTASIES

Life's a day at the beach for the shore-loving resident of this sunny room. Jaunty beach balls abound on the wallpaper and furniture, and stuffed fabric balls decorate the desk, hang from the wall, and adorn the ties atop the window treatment. Sand pails and a picnic at the beach are the subjects of framed pictures on the desk and wall.

DESIGN: DAWN KEARNEY, DESIGN LINE INTERIORS, INC.

A magical rocking horse cabinet, inspired by a contemporary myth, is paired with a mirror frame made from baby blocks, seashells, marbles, and model cars.

DESIGN: TAD TAYLOR'S FANTASY FURNTIURE

DESIGN: DEE THELAN INTERIORS.
DECORATIVE PAINTING: SUZANNE STRACHAN, ARTISTIC EFFECTS

The Old West comes to life in a shared room containing thematic bedding, Native American-style bedspreads and rugs, an intricately tooled saddle, lassos, and models of horses, covered wagons, stagecoaches, and tepees.

Fantasy bunk beds in the form of a medieval castle (at left) are decorated in ice-cream colors suitable for boys or girls. A young boy's field of dreams (below) is filled with baseball paraphernalia—baseballs for bedpost finials, and bats for drawer pulls and balusters on the bed and nightstand.

DESIGN: JUVENILE LIFESTYLES, INC.

DESIGN: CAROL SILVERMAN & ASSOCIATES ENVIRONMENTAL DESIGN.
DECORATIVE PAINTING: SUZANNE STRACHAN, ARTISTIC EFFECTS.

A hand-painted mural of exotic wildlife and lush vegetation transports the human occupant of this room to the inner reaches of an African jungle. The bedspread simulates animal skin.

DESIGN: CYNTHIA BRIAN OF STARSTYLE INTERIORS

In this little girl's floral fantasy, delicate blossoms and bows bedeck the walls, window treatment, bedding, canopy, and furniture. Stuffed animals conduct their own tea party at the child-size wicker table and chairs.

DESIGN: TAD TAYLOR'S FANTASY FURNITURE

A fantasy bed resembling a little cottage is set against rolling hills. Bright colors and simple lines make the room look as if it popped out of a cartoon or comic book.

DESIGN: EURODESIGN, LTD.

This efficient wall unit (at left) incorporates open shelving, cabinets, drawers, and a corner desk. The chest bed drawers provide additional storage. A built-in wall unit (below) contains plentiful open and concealed storage. A library ladder securely attached to a track invites kids to use high shelves.

A PLACE FOR EVERYTHING

ARCHITECTS HRIBAR & WHIPPLE

DESIGN: FUN FURNITURE

A whimsical high-rise building and little house serve as both playthings and storage units. The front of the building opens up and the house roof pops off to divulge stowage space.

A PLACE FOR
EVERYTHING

Hooks, wall racks, and coat racks are often sufficient to accommodate the few toddler clothes that require hanging. Here, a decorative wall rack holds a little girl's Sunday-best wardrobe.

Constructing an open-back bookcase around and below the window created generous storage and display space in this small room.

To clean up the clutter, this closet was fitted with adjustable shelving, vinyl-coated wire bins, and two levels of rods. The youngster responsible for maintaining order can easily see at a glance where everything belongs.

An antique wardrobe to which shelves have been added holds books, toys, games, and stuffed animals. The doors can be closed when company comes.

READING & WRITING

This sleek white laminate desk with overhead shelving makes a shipshape study center. The thick shelves are actually laminate-covered plywood boxes.

DESIGN: CALVIN L. SMITH ASSOCIATES, INC.

A built-in, cushioned bench is a cozy place to curl up and read a good storybook—and, later on, school texts. Here, a youngster snuggles up with stuffed friends.

DESIGN: CAROL SPONG, ASID

This drop-front desk swings down to reveal cubby holes and a surface just the right size for penning letters. When closed, it maintains a slim, neat profile. The desk was painted to match the adjacent wall unit incorporating a wardrobe, chest of drawers, and entertainment center.

*An authentic-looking tepee (at left) is
the perfect hideout for a youngster seek-
ing solitude, and a great place to hold
pow-wows with friends. This beguiling
fantasy (below) beckons kids to
climb a magical tree, explore a troll's
cave, and slide down the back
of a friendly dragon.*

H IDEOUTS

ARCHITECTS: STEVEN FOOTE PERRY DEAN ROGERS & PARTNERS

Stair treads poking through a faux stone walkway lead to what looks like a house facade attached to the upper wall in a room corner. It's no fake— the front swings opens to a cozy, cushioned hideaway (detail at top).

DESIGN: PALMER/PLETSCH ASSOCIATES

A colorful circus-motif tent canopy and flaps attach to bunk beds, allowing kids to play and sleep under the big top.

Little kids love climbing into snug spaces, such as the crannies in this carpeted climbing structure. The nooks and ledges are also great places to display toys.

ARCHITECTS: COORDT & CO., ARCHITECTURE • PLANNING

Solitude is only a ladder's climb away for the kids who share these high-ceilinged sleeping quarters. As shown in the detail at right, a visitor to the loft can pull down the window shade for extra privacy.

ARCHITECTS: RIVKIN WEISMAN

SWEET DREAMS

An overhead shelf and wallpaper border help define the sleeping area in a bedroom (at right) made serene by an imaginative use of soft colors. The cleverly designed loft bed (below) is actually half of an inverted Victorian four-poster positioned over modular cabinetry and shelving.

DESIGN: DAVID RIVERA DESIGNS, INC.

Built on an irregularly shaped platform, this young musician's custom bed is close to all the action—drums, stereo system, and books. The carpeted lower step is an inviting place to lounge and visit with friends.

DESIGN: AMERICAN WOOD COUNCIL

A built-in captain's bed makes a snug sleeping nook for a child. Shelves at the head and foot hold all the nighttime necessities.

DECORATING DETAILS

A flower-lined path leads to a
turreted castle occupied by storybook
characters. Who would guess that
such an enchanting facade conceals
a wall bed?

DESIGN: M. ENID ARCKLESS, ASID, MEA DESIGNS

DESIGN: KATHERINE WALDEN, DECORATIVE PAINTING: AUDREY P. RABY

The area rug and furniture were hand-
painted to create a rich, ornate look in
a little girl's Victorian-style room.

A skirted, glass-top dressing table and
upholstered footstool set against a
winsome mural lend old-fashioned
charm to this room. The picture
frames, lamps, and knickknacks were
chosen for their intricate detailing.

*The picket fence (at right) frames
the view from the nursery window,
merging indoors and outdoors.
Careful attention was paid to color
in this attic bedroom (below):
yellows, magentas, and blues in
various tints and shades are
repeated throughout the room.*

DESIGN: HEIDI EMMETT

WINDOW TREATMENT: ROSETTI & CORRIEA DRAPERIES, INC.

A predominantly pastel color scheme (above) creates a restful feeling conducive to quiet play. A green, yellow, and white color scheme punctuated with a checkerboard trim (at right) distinguish this sunny closet.

Fancifully painted scenes make magic in an attic nursery. A faux skylight brings cheer to the room, even during gloomy weather. The lamp and books atop the dresser aren't real, since the chest is recessed into the wall. Adding to the air of enchantment are rabbits disappearing into a warren (really just a door leading to a storage area).

DESIGN: ANN CARTER

DESIGN: ICKEN ASSOCIATES, INC.

GREAT KIDS' ROOMS   **69**

A SHOPPER'S GUIDE

Look at the fanciful, colorful furnishings available for children today, and you'll wish you were a kid again! The options include loft beds that look like castles, chest beds with built-in storage bins, whimsical wardrobes, kid-size chairs and sofas, game-board rugs, cushiony three-dimensional wall hangings, and decorating kits with repositionable borders and appliqués in kid-pleasing motifs. And that's just the beginning.

This chapter tells you what products are available and where to find many of them. It will help you to transform your child's room into a special refuge for dreaming, lounging, studying, playing, and entertaining friends.

An antique brass headboard and a quilted comforter with a colorful undersea motif are the starting points for a young girl's room decor. Now various wallpaper, paint, fabric, and carpet samples are being considered for suitability.

BEDS

Most babies start out in a crib or, for the first few months, in the cozier confines of a cradle or bassinet. A youngster is ready for a bed, either intermediate or adult-size, when he or she attains a height of about 35 inches or repeatedly climbs out of the crib.

Choose carefully. Children spend a lot of time sleeping, so it's important to provide a safe, comfortable sleep surface that supports their growing bodies in a healthful way. Also remember that to a child a bed is more than just a place for slumber. It's a gymnasium, where infants develop motor skills and young kids release pent-up energy. Later on, it's a place for lounging, reading, and seating friends.

The most common beds sold for kids' rooms are described here. Usually, you purchase the mattress separately; see page 75 for tips on choosing a good one.

INFANT BEDS

Safety is the most important consideration in buying this type of bed. You're sure to find something in your budget, since prices start from under $100 (as low as $40 for a no-frills bassinet) and range upward to several hundred dollars, depending on style, materials, and other options. Infants grow so fast that secondhand bedding can give excellent value.

As all but the most starry-eyed first-time parents know, all materials should be washable. And on an older piece of furniture, be sure any paint is lead-free.

Cradles & Bassinets

These tiny beds are popular alternatives to cribs for the first two or three months of life. Their snug size is supposedly comforting to newborns. But once your infant is ready to roll over, such restricted sleeping quarters are no longer safe. Also, these little beds are equipped with only a pad (it should be at least 2 inches thick), and a baby soon needs the firmer support of a mattress.

Since neither cradles nor bassinets are completely regulated, you'll have to take on the responsibility of checking safety features.

Choose a cradle with the highest sides possible to hold the baby securely when the bed is rocked. For safety, the rockers should curve only slightly, moving with a gentle motion. On a suspended cradle, look for a sturdy base, secure pivoting hardware, and a design that lets you lock the cradle in a nonswinging position.

Because of its large size, the European-style cradle at left accommodates babies a few months longer than most cradles would. Pretty wicker bassinet (above) sits securely in its frame and contains ample padding.

A stable base is also critical in a bassinet, which is a basketlike bed (often with a hood at one end) atop a stand that may or may not have wheels. The basket and frame may be a single unit, or the basket may lift off the stand—if it does, make sure the handles are firmly attached to the frame. A wicker model should have no protruding reeds.

Cribs

Most cribs made since 1990 conform to current safety rules; make sure a secondhand or custom-made crib meets these standards before using it.

Slats should be spaced no more than 2⅜ inches apart, corner posts or finials should be no higher than ¹⁄₁₆ inch (canopy and other posts higher than 16 inches don't count), and the mattress should fit snugly with less than two fingers' width between the crib sides and mattress. Any cutouts in the headboard or footboard should be small enough so no part of the baby's body can be trapped in them.

The latching mechanisms that release the drop side should be well out of the baby's reach and require dual action or at least 10 pounds of pressure for release.

Check for tight supports, screws, and bolts. A toddler can be very active, jumping up and down in the crib, so solid construction is especially important.

To discourage a baby from climbing out, the distance between the mattress and the top of the rails should be as great as possible. Methods for lowering mattresses vary. Some cribs have only two levels, while others have three or four. With some, you simply move levers, while others necessitate unbolting, repositioning the bottom support, and rebolting.

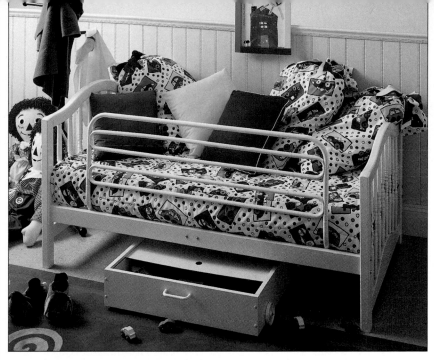

An intermediate bed, such as this one with a detachable guardrail, will sleep a youngster from about age 2 to 5.

You can buy a crib with built-in storage or a convertible type. On some models, the rail on one side can be removed to create a day bed, or both side rails can be detached to make a toddler bed. On other models, you can remove the rails and add a mattress extender to lengthen the sleeping area by about 16 inches; the extender covers an area previously occupied by a chest of drawers, which you now move to the side.

The disadvantages of a convertible crib are that it costs more, you may need the crib for another baby, and the lengthened bed is soon outgrown—especially if your youngster refuses to sleep in a "baby bed" and demands an adult bed.

INTERMEDIATE BEDS

Sometimes called toddler, junior, or youth beds, these units are suitable for a relatively short time, usually between the ages of 2 and 5. The

Cribs are available in many styles and materials. This brass model features a colorful canopy and matching bedding and bumpers.

bed may not even last that long if your child thinks it's too babyish and wants a "real bed."

Many parents view intermediate beds as wasteful because of their short life span. Doting relatives sometimes buy one to keep for a visiting child.

In addition to beds that convert from cribs, many types are sold solely as intermediate beds. Some are fantasy beds (see page 77), while others look like miniature versions of adult beds, except that the mattress sits directly on slats and guardrails may be attached to the frame.

There is no standard size: some of these beds can take a crib mattress (though you may need your old one for another baby), and some require a slightly larger mattress. You may have a hard time finding a mattress and bedding for an odd-size model.

You can buy a simple, tubular steel bed frame for about $50, a fantasy race car frame for about $150.

ADULT-SIZE BEDS

A standard adult bed consists of a frame, mattress, and box spring or other support. The frame may be just a plain metal support on casters or may include a headboard and/or footboard. Some beds are categorized by their frame's design—for example, a four-poster bed. Standard beds come in twin, full, queen, and king sizes, although twin is most often used in kids' rooms. If your child is destined to be tall, you may want to purchase an extra-long model, if available, or invest in a custom bed.

When moving a toddler from a crib to an adult bed, use a guardrail to keep the child from falling out. You'll find detachable models made of metal, plastic, or nylon mesh.

On the following pages, we review common types of adult-size beds sold for kids' rooms. What you'll pay depends on design, quality, materials, and other options. Because of the number of components involved, loft beds are usually the priciest. You can get a sturdy loft setup with a bed, guardrail, ladder, armoire, bookcase, and desk for a little under $1,000—or you can spend several times that amount. A wall bed can cost more than $1,000, but most other styles are priced from about $200 to $800. In most cases, the mattress (and box spring, if needed) are extra.

Bunk Beds

These are classic space savers when you're doubling up kids in a room—and even if there's only one child, a second bunk can provide extra play space and accommodation for an overnight guest. Keep in mind that the

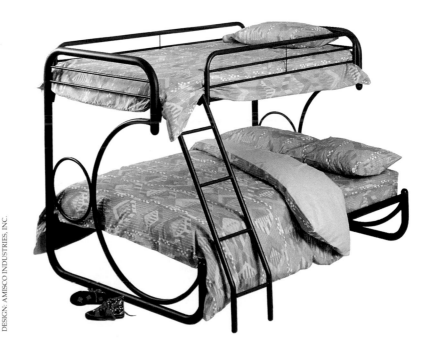

The sturdy wood-frame bunks (at left), with end rails that serve as a ladder, can be unstacked and used as twin beds if desired. The metal-frame pyramid bunk (above), with a double bed on bottom and a twin bed on top, is designed for stacking mode only.

top bunk will be awkward to make, and that its occupant could swelter on hot nights if the room does not have good ventilation. Also realize that some kids aren't happy about heights.

Conventional bunks stack directly on top of each other, and the most practical models can be unstacked and used as twin beds. A less common configuration consists of an L-shaped arrangement of freestanding beds, with one placed partially under the other. For the greatest versatility, get a unit that can function as stacking bunks, L-bunks, or twin beds. Some manufacturers sell kits that can convert bunks into loft units.

A relatively recent option is a pyramid or stair-step bunk, consisting of a full bed below and a twin bed above.

Some conventional bunk beds allow you to slip either a mattress or a desktop insert into the top of the lower bunk. Your child can use the bottom unit as a desk most of the time, but by adding the mattress, convert it to a bed for an overnight guest.

Examine bunks carefully before you buy. Look for solid construction, with no wobbling when the beds are stacked. The spacing of rails should be narrow enough so a child's head can't accidentally be caught between them. The upper unit should have a sturdy guardrail—one on each side, if the bed isn't placed against a wall. Be sure the mattress is at least 5 inches below the guardrail's upper edge. The ladder, if not integral, should attach securely to the top bunk and be easy for children to climb.

Usually, the mattress rests over slats; in many cases, you can get a thin wooden panel to lay over the slats, so the child in the lower bunk can't kick or poke the mattress of the upper unit.

Not all bunk beds are the same height. Be certain there's adequate headroom for both occupants.

Loft Beds

These elevated beds maximize floor space. Types for young children often incorporate a fantasy motif, such as a castle, and feature a play area underneath. Models intended to see kids into adulthood usually include a desk, with drawers and other storage below. Some manufacturers offer a matching twin bed that goes under the loft to form an L-shaped bunk.

BUYING A MATTRESS

Even though kids may not weigh as much as adults, they need good, firm sleep support just as much as adults do. The technical information provided here can help you select a good mattress. But remember, the deciding factor should be comfort. If your child is too young to make the decision about an adult-size mattress, stretch out on the various models yourself. That's better than relying on product labels, since one manufacturer's "firm" may feel harder than another's "extra-firm."

Innerspring mattresses are the type most commonly sold. Look for more than 100 coils in a crib mattress, more than 200 in a twin mattress, and more than 300 in a full-size model. A high coil count isn't the whole story, though. Wire gauge is also important—the lower the number, the stronger the wire, with 13 the heaviest gauge and 21 the lightest. Also, the more layers of quality cushioning and insulation provided, the more comfortable the mattress will prove.

A high-quality foam mattress is just as good as a well-constructed innerspring mattress. Foam mattresses can consist of a solid core of foam or of several layers of different types of foam laminated together. The traditional latex (synthetic rubber) and the newer high-resilience polyurethanes are among the highest-performance foams. Generally, the higher the density, the better the foam. Be sure to get a mini-

mum density of at least 1.15 pounds per cubic foot in a crib mattress or 2 pounds per cubic foot in an adult-size mattress.

Most beds intended for adults accommodate a box spring to support the mattress and add more comfort. However, the majority of adult-size beds sold in kids' shops are designed for the mattress to rest directly over slats or a wood panel; using a box spring on these beds would make them too high for the frame and wouldn't permit trundle or drawer options under the bed. You can expect a mattress on a rigid support to wear out faster than one on a box spring.

The average cost for good-quality mattresses is as follows: crib mattresses about $90; twin mattresses $150 to $190; and full-size mattresses $250 to $275, plus about a third again as much for a box spring.

STANDARD MATTRESS DIMENSIONS

Bed Size	Width		Length
Crib	28"	X	52"
Twin	39"	X	75"
Extra-long twin	39"	X	80"
Full	54"	X	75"

Most loft beds are best used where ceilings are higher than 8 feet, so be sure there will be enough room for the child to study or play under the loft as well as adequate headroom above. Lower lofts are usually intended for young kids. They often have a slide or a tented area underneath that looks like a playhouse or fort. Some short lofts have a pull-out desk that stores below.

The standard loft has a twin bed, but you can also find models with extra-long twin, full, or queen beds. Most lofts are made of wood. Better-made fantasy types have steel frames, while less expensive ones are made entirely of particleboard.

Trundle Beds

This space-saving unit pulls out from underneath another bed to accommodate a sibling or an overnight guest. The standard size is twin.

Some trundles are freestanding units on casters, while others sit on attached frames. Many modular furniture lines feature beds with matching trundle units. You can even get trundles for some bunk beds.

Be sure the trundle draws out smoothly, and that your child can handle it alone—unless you want to do the pulling every time it's used.

Captain's & Chest Beds

As the term implies, a captain's bed is named for the built-in units used by ships' captains. It usually contains at least two rows of drawers. Some models have shallow cabinets flanked by sets of double drawers. An authentic-looking captain's bed has high sides—on a ship, they prevent the occupant from being tossed out during rough weather.

A chest bed may feature built-in drawers or a trundle, or both. Models designed for younger children have compartments for toys. The configuration of storage areas varies from one manufacturer to another.

Captain's and chest beds sleep a little higher than standard beds because they incorporate storage below. To make room for this, the mattress sits on slats or a wood panel.

Canopy Beds

Marketed primarily for girls, canopy beds have an overhead framework and often a roof-like covering. Some come with drawers or a trundle below.

DESIGN: EURODESIGN, LTD.

Rustic loft (top) leaves plenty of space for play below. Sleek chest bed (bottom) contains two drawers for clothes or toy storage and a trundle bed for overnight guests.

Although many canopy beds can be assembled on site, some can't—so be sure the bed will fit through the doorway before you buy. Also make sure the ceiling is high enough so the bed doesn't overpower the space.

Wall Beds

These disappearing beds swing up into a cabinet or wall unit, freeing floor space for play or hobbies. The mattress and bedding are secured with straps so they stay put when the bed is raised.

Although this type of bed opens up a small room during the daytime, it's difficult for young children to operate on their own, and may make a child's quarters seem less personal.

Fantasy Beds

These whimsical beds come in such shapes as racing cars, airplanes, sailboats, and teddy bears. Although some fantasy beds take a crib mattress, those accommodating a twin size have a longer life. You can even get a fantasy bed in the form of a bunk or loft.

The beds range from fairly inexpensive plastic types to more costly and elaborate models made from wood or steel upholstered with foam and canvas. If the motif you want isn't available ready-made, you can order a custom design.

If you want a bed to serve your child longer, consider getting a standard bed with a fantasy facade bolted to the frame. The facade can be removed when the child outgrows the fantasy. If you're handy, you can make the facade yourself by cutting a sheet of plywood in the shape of the desired motif and painting it or covering it with fabric.

The decorative canopy bed (top) creates a dainty milieu; the wall bed (middle) saves space in a small room; and the fantasy bed (bottom) appeals to a young rail fan.

DESIGN: LANDS' END

DESIGN: EURODESIGN, LTD.

DESIGN: CLOCKWORK INTERIORS

TABLES, DESKS & SEATING

Adults work, play, and lounge in other rooms of the house, but kids do all of that in their bedrooms, and they need furniture to accommodate these activities. This section describes work surfaces—from changing tables to computer desks—and seating that kids' rooms need.

Make sure the table or desk you choose is the right height for your child; its top should reach mid-thigh level when the child is standing. See the chart on page 26.

Chairs used for long periods for crafts projects or homework should provide good back support. Your child's feet should rest flat on the floor, and there should be a gap of several inches between young knees and the underside of the table or desk.

Changing Tables

You can change a baby on any stable surface with raised sides and, preferably, a safety strap. Changing tables range from about $50 to several hundred dollars.

The most common design resembles a small shelving unit. The baby goes in the top enclosure, and supplies are stored in shelves underneath. Depending on the model, the table may or may not be able to work as a bookcase or storage unit later on.

Some manufacturers incorporate changing tables as part of wardrobes and dressers. The most versatile ones can be converted to shelving for toys or some other use as the child grows. Some companies sell the flip-top separately. Be wary of any that sits too close to the edge of a dresser; although heavy, it still can be accidentally knocked off.

DESIGN: COSCO

DESIGN: JUVENILE LIFESTYLES, INC.

DESIGN: SAMSON McCANN

Changing table (top left) features a safety rail and restraint belt for baby's protection. The top surface and interior of bedside table (lower left) are spacious enough to hold all the items a youngster needs at bedtime. Benches and base of the adjustable table (above) rotate to three different heights to accommodate youngsters until about age 11.

It isn't really necessary to invest in a separate piece of furniture. If you prefer, you can just buy a mat or portable changing tray to fit on top of an existing piece of furniture.

Bedside Tables

Unless storage is built into the bed's headboard, your child will need some kind of table to hold a lamp, clock, tissues, and other necessities. It's useful to have a shelf or two for books or toys.

You don't have to get a unit sold specifically as a bedside table or nightstand. A low bookcase can work just as well, and even a large storage cube will do. Whatever your choice, just be sure that your child can reach the top surface easily from the bed.

A bedside table isn't practical in some cases, as with a loft bed or the top level of bunk beds. A clip-on light clamped to the headboard or post is one way to provide illumination for these, and lamps, clock radios, and tissue boxes are all available in wall-mounted models; just hang a pocket for a bedtime book. You could also affix a narrow shelf to the wall.

Low Tables & Chairs

Little kids love tables and chairs their own size that they can snuggle into. A diminutive set, available plain or in whimsical designs, will last until your child is about 6 years old. You can pay as little as $50 for molded plastic or as much as several hundred dollars for fancifully painted wood.

Sturdiness is a major consideration, since kids are sure to use the set in ways you never dreamed of, jumping on the tabletop and playing underneath inverted chairs. Children sometimes want their parents to sit with them, so be sure the chairs will bear your weight.

The safest sets have smooth, rounded edges, not sharp ones. Washability is also key, since your child is likely to get crayon marks and paint smears on the surface.

Tables and chairs are available in various heights. If you buy a set, the chairs will be scaled to the table's height—not necessarily the case when you buy them separately. You can replace the legs of some tables with longer ones as your child grows. You can't do the same with chairs, however.

Study Desks

Many types of desks and tables, available in a wide price range, are suitable for schoolwork. Most are stationary, but some fold away or adjust in height as the child grows. Others are incorporated into bunk and loft structures.

Most feature drawers, which are handy for storing little items. Some offer desktop hutches as an option. Surfaces vary in size, so be sure you choose one big enough so your child can spread books and papers out comfortably.

You can make your own desk by fixing a piece of painted plywood or even an old flat door on top of low bookcases or stackable drawers or bins. Or attach a work surface directly to wall studs with sturdy hardware.

DESIGN: DESIGN HORIZONS BY LADD FURNITURE, INC.

Tucked under the white melamine drafting desk (at left) is a rolling cabinet with a drawer front that reverses to white. The height and back support of the chair are adjustable. The modular study center (below), featuring a black melamine surface and wood-veneer drawer fronts, has a computer desk with a pull-out keyboard tray. Hand-painting has transformed a simple wood folding chair into an accent piece.

DESIGN: JUVENILE LIFESTYLES, INC.

SHOPPING FOR FURNITURE

Children's furniture comes in a variety of styles, materials, and quality levels. Prices run a gamut, too. Don't expect good furniture to cost less just because it's for kids.

Even if your budget can accommodate pricey items, you may want to avoid them. If your child is rough with belongings, don't buy the best and expect a sudden change in behavior. Get sturdy but less costly items, and you won't feel as disappointed if they're treated roughly.

To stretch a budget, look for furniture that can be raised, added onto, or reconfigured as a child grows. Other practical choices are pieces that convert to other uses when the child outgrows the original plan.

For the best selection, check kids' shops, general furniture stores, department stores, home-improvement centers, and specialty catalogs. Many high-end and custom items are available through interior designers.

For tips on buying specific types of furniture, refer to the rest of this chapter. Generally, look for solid construction, since kids can use furniture in unpredictable ways. There shouldn't be any splinters, ragged edges, or exposed nails or other hardware to harm children. Rounded corners are a good safety feature. Check drawers, doors, and other moving parts for smooth, safe operation.

Materials

The quality, life expectancy, and cost of a piece of furniture are related to the material of which it is made. The following are some commonly used materials. You'll also find wicker, metal, and molded plastic items.

Wood. A piece of furniture can be made of solid wood, wood veneer over plywood panels, or a combination. Solid wood is more durable, richer looking, and costlier than veneer, although veneered panels are less apt to warp.

Woods are either hardwood (from deciduous trees) or softwood (from conifers). Common hardwoods used for furniture include oak, ash, beech, birch, maple, cherry, and walnut. Hardwoods make more precise joints, hold fasteners better, are more resistant to wear, and generally cost more than softwoods. Common softwoods are pine and fir, used primarily in unfinished furniture.

Composition Board. The two main types used for kids' furniture are particleboard and medium-density fiberboard (MDF)—both are less expensive than solid wood or good-quality plywood, but are also weaker and more likely to chip.

Particleboard is made from very small pieces of wood bonded together, while MDF is a stiffer material made from compressed wood fibers. Both are used as a substrate for laminates. MDF also takes paint well.

MDF costs more than particleboard; its uniform texture allows it to be milled like wood. It's popular with makers of juvenile furniture because it can be cut into fanciful shapes that are smooth all over, even at cut ends. By contrast, particleboard's pocked ends must usually be laminated or hidden in some other way.

Laminates. These popular surfacing materials for kids' furniture are tough, easy to clean, and available in a wide range of colors.

Of the three major surfacing materials, high-pressure plastic laminate is by far the most durable, and also the costliest. Melamine, a surface layer of resin-impregnated paper, is less expensive but very serviceable. The lowest grade is vinyl or paper surface film, which is thin and can peel away.

Computer Desks

Desks designed to hold a home computer system usually feature a hutch top with shelves and ledges to hold components. The desk may be a single unit, or the pedestal and hutch may be sold separately. Prices range from under $100 to several times that amount. Such a desk is of limited use for other tasks, since the computer equipment and supplies take up most of the available space.

Make sure that the position of the monitor and keyboard is suitable for your child. The monitor should be at eye level, and the keyboard lower than standard desk level to avoid stress on the wrists. If the desk top isn't slightly lower than a standard desk, there should be a slide-out keyboard tray at a lower height.

You can set up computer equipment on a regular desk. Some makers of modular furniture offer a keyboard tray that you can affix to the underside of the desk.

Desk Chairs

Some of the most common types are secretarial chairs, folding metal chairs, and straight-back chairs.

Some options for scaled-down seating are shown here. Clockwise from top left they include miniature reproduction of a Queen Anne chair, aniline-dyed wood chair, tubular metal and fabric rocker, dinosaur-motif combination stool and chair, wicker rocker, convertible sofa, small director's chair, rush and wood chair, hickory rocker, and larger director's chair resting on a bean bag.

The one that will last your child the longest is the secretarial chair, since both the seat height and back support are adjustable. Most secretarial chairs roll on casters and are easy to move; the five-footed pedestal gives greatest stability. Generally, the better the upholstery and the more adjustable the chair, the higher the price. A caution: some kids prefer swiveling to studying, so keep that in mind if your child is easily distracted.

Folding metal chairs and straight-back chairs aren't likely to offer as much comfort for long-term sitting or support the back as well.

Folding chairs come in many colors, while straight-back types are most often wood. The seats of either may be hard or padded. Depending on its heft, a straight-back chair may be difficult for a young child to move. Prices range from about $10 for a simple folding chair to several hundred dollars for a fine wooden piece.

Occasional Seating

Adult-size chairs are fine for older kids, but younger ones find the scale overwhelming. They're happier in seating their own size.

Many manufacturers of kids' furniture make scaled-down seating suitable for children until about age 5. You'll find little stools, director's chairs, folding wood chairs, and rockers priced between $10 and $70 at shops selling children's furniture. Pint-size, foam-filled easy chairs and couches, some of which convert into sleeping space for young guests, retail for $50 to $150. Inexpensive bean bags and floor pillows are other options, appealing to kids of all ages.

High-end furniture showrooms sometimes stock such items as bantam-size reproductions of Queen Anne chairs and diminutive wicker chairs and loveseats. These pricey pieces are often available only through designers, and may not be the most practical choices even where budgets permit.

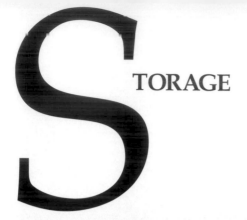

STORAGE

The burgeoning world of storage containers includes plastic bins, tubs, crates, boxes, and jars, plus mesh hammocks, string bags, cardboard boxes, canvas toy chests, wall racks, hanging pockets, hatboxes, and metal lockers. Even storage items intended for other uses can go to work in a kid's room —a vacuum cleaner attachment holder is a great way to store baseball equipment.

Unlike adults' bedrooms, kids' rooms need places to stow not just clothes but also toys, games, puzzles, books, stuffed animals, cherished collections, and other assorted treasures.

Storage units come in myriad forms, from large pieces of furniture to little boxes and bins. They're made of various materials, including wood, composition board, wicker, metal, plastic, and fabric. Prices are just as wide-ranging.

Shop for storage units as you would for any kind of furniture (see page 80). Look for solid construction and durability, and for surfaces that can easily be cleaned. Also make sure that there are no sharp edges that could hurt young users.

Closet Systems

Not only do most bedroom closets waste space, but they're not intended for little kids—the pole and shelf are too high. Luckily, there are easy ways to modify closets to make them more useful.

The best solution is a modular system that will meet the changing needs of a developing child. Poles can be raised, shelves rearranged, and more drawers or hanging space added as the child grows.

You can organize the closet yourself. Home-improvement centers and specialty shops sell components, including poles, shelves, cabinets, stacking drawers, wire baskets, and hooks. Most closet shops also design and install custom systems.

Another option is to hire an independent contractor who specializes in organizing closets. Look for one who has done children's closets before and shows some understanding of a child's storage needs.

A closet system maximizes storage space in a child's room. This slatted shelving system, available through many closet shops and storage contractors, is made of handsome hardwood.

A fully developed system can cost from under $100 to thousands of dollars, depending on the closet size, the number and variety of components (generally, drawers are the most expensive units), and the quality of the materials. Price systems carefully: you may find that some custom systems are nearly as economical as do-it-yourself arrangements, and a whole lot easier if you're not especially handy with tools.

Wardrobes

A wardrobe offers convenient clothes storage if the room has no closet or an inadequate one, or if the closet is being used for another purpose.

Since young children don't have many clothes that need hanging, child-size armoires are usually fitted with more drawers or shelves than hanging space. Although they can be charming, these armoires are quickly

outgrown—and may cost more than you want to spend.

An adult wardrobe will last longer, but may contain too much hanging space to suit your child's needs. You could modify the interior by adding shelves along one side. Move the pole down to your child's eye level, and gradually raise it as the child grows. Add appeal to an inexpensive, plain unit by painting or wallpapering it inside or out.

Dressers

A chest of drawers stores clothes that can be folded, but it can also hold toys and other items. You can pay less than $100 for a no-frills but functional unit or several times that for a decorative piece of fine furniture.

If you want a young child to be in charge of the dresser, make sure he or she is capable of using it. The child should be able to reach the top draw-

DESIGN: VISADOR COMPANY

er without standing on a stool or other prop, and to grasp pulls easily to open and close the drawers.

Look for sturdy construction and stability. The dresser shouldn't be so top-heavy that it tips over when the upper drawer is pulled out. For safety, each drawer should move on glides equipped with stops to keep it from coming all the way out.

If the closet is large enough, you could place the dresser inside, or even plan one into a closet system (see page 83).

For a very young child, consider a modular system with stacking drawers; you can add more units as the child grows.

Under-bed Drawers

Easy for a child to reach, drawers under the bed frame provide handy storage for clothing and toys. They're the perfect solution for kids who like to tidy up by throwing everything under the bed.

Some beds, such as chest types, feature built-in drawers. The number and dimensions of drawers vary among manufacturers.

Many modular furniture lines offer freestanding drawers on casters that slide under the bed. Usually two drawers, sitting side by side, fit under a bed. Or you can opt for a trundle frame on casters and use it as one gigantic drawer. You'll pay anywhere from about $100 to $400 for a set of drawers or a trundle frame.

Some mail-order catalogs sell rolling drawers, approximately 2 feet square, made of laminated composition board—some with open tops, some with lids—or wire mesh. A set of two costs about $30 to $60.

Clothes Hampers

For a couple of hundred dollars, you can buy a kids' clothes hamper in the shape of a house or other fanciful form. If that seems too extravagant, one or more large wicker baskets with lids will do the same job for a fraction of the cost.

Another relatively inexpensive choice is a basketball hoop with a long net that can be closed at the bottom. Although not the most attractive solution, it does encourage kids to pick up dirty clothes, if only so they can toss them into the hoop. Just make sure the hoop is emptied frequently.

Bookcases & Shelving Units

Available in all sizes, from small decorative ledges to large wall systems, these units are great for storing or displaying books, toys, collectibles, and other items. Prices depend on size, style, and materials.

Modular pieces let you increase storage or display space as needed. Adjustable shelves make it easy to keep pace with a growing child. Be sure shelves are sturdy enough to bear the weight of their expected load; the lighter the weight, the wider the span you can get away with.

DESIGN: BOSTON AND WINTHROP

DESIGN: FISHER-PRICE

Under-bed drawers (at left) roll out for easy access to clothes, toys, or extra bedding. Chest of drawers (above) is customized with painted pulls and stenciled pinwheels.

Open shelving lets children see where things belong and encourages them to return things to their rightful places. Cabinet doors at the bottom of a unit that rests on the floor will discourage little kids from climbing up—and can also store some odds and ends out of sight.

For safety's sake, don't put a glass-fronted case in a young child's room. Anchor any freestanding unit to the wall if it's the least bit unsteady.

Toy Chests

Some boxes are designed especially to hold toys. Many also can serve as child-size benches or low tables.

Look for one with safety hinges that prevent the lid from falling shut. Another desirable safety feature is an air opening just under the closed lid (in case the child gets trapped inside). Some manufacturers are abandoning lids altogether and making uncovered toy boxes.

Most lidded boxes are priced between $50 and $150. An uncovered chest can cost as little as $30.

Bins, Boxes & Baskets

An easy, economical way to organize toys and games is to sort them in plastic, laminated, cardboard, wire-mesh, or wicker containers. You'll find them in assorted sizes, shapes, colors, and prices in home-improvement centers, hardware stores, specialty shops, and mail-order catalogs.

Look for storage units that have smooth edges, are easy for your child to handle, and will stand up to abuse. Many units are stackable and can be added to as your child's storage needs increase.

Color-coding the bins, boxes, and baskets will help children remember where things go. For example, you can wrap plain cardboard boxes in brightly colored self-adhesive paper.

This folding cabinet is designed as classroom furniture, but most manufacturers will sell such items directly to parents. The unit features adjustable shelves and sturdy casters for easy rolling.

DESIGN: WHITNEY BROTHERS

DESIGN: FUN FURNITURE

The toy chest in the shape of a house has a safety hinge to keep the lid from slamming shut. The one in the form of a yellow taxi is an open chest that doubles as a toy car that toddlers can wheel around the room.

FLOORING

Flooring in kids' rooms, especially those of young children, should break a fall without breaking bones, provide a good surface for play and other activities, and clean up easily.

Resilient Floors

This category includes floors made from vinyl, rubber, and cork—materi- als that have supplanted linoleum, a type of resilient flooring no longer manufactured in the United States.

Available in many colors, tex- tures, patterns, and styles, resilient floors are flexible underfoot, yet firm, durable, sound-absorbing, and easy to maintain. A protective finish applied at the factory eliminates the need for waxing. A textured material can hide dust and guard against slipping, but doesn't provide a smooth surface for play.

Sheet goods are sold in rolls up to 12 feet wide; most tiles are 12 inches square. Resilient flooring requires a smooth underlayment, since it molds to any irregularities in the subfloor.

Vinyl. Most resilient flooring is made of vinyl. Sheet goods come with an inlaid or printed pattern (inlaid wears better), with or without a cushioned backing (cushioning is more comfort- able underfoot but dents more easily).

Vinyl tiles don't generally wear as well as sheet goods, but they offer cer- tain advantages: you can mix different tiles to form custom patterns or pro- vide color accents; you can install them yourself quite easily (if you get self-stick tiles); and you can replace tiles in damaged areas without replac- ing the whole floor.

Commercial vinyl composition tiles are a good choice for kids' rooms. They're nearly indestructible, and the

color goes all the way through, masking scrapes and scratches. They're also economical, ranging from less than $1 to about $2 per square foot. On the down side, these tiles don't have a no-wax surface, and patterns are limited. However, they come in a wide range of solid colors, allowing you to create intriguing designs of your own.

There's no need to buy the considerably more expensive solid vinyl or luxury vinyl tiles unless you want a particular pattern—many of which simulate other materials, such as hardwood, slate, or marble. Color goes all the way through a solid vinyl tile, but the pattern is either printed on the surface and protected with a no-wax finish or is molded into the tile surface during the production process and doesn't have a protective finish. Luxury vinyl isn't necessary solid; the term just denotes a high-priced product.

Rubber. Sold in large tiles (approximately 18 inches square), rubber flooring is more often used commercially than in homes. The choice of colors and patterns is much more limited than for vinyl tiles. You'll also pay more for rubber than for vinyl composition tiles—$5 per square foot and up.

Although popular in kitchens, rubber floors with studs or other raised patterns aren't the most practical choice for kids' rooms. The resulting surface is too bumpy for some activities, and dirt tends to build up around the studs.

Resilient flooring (opposite page) is a sensible choice for a young child's room. Here is a sampling of vinyl tiles and sheet goods, including some simulating wood. Genuine wood (at right) is another good option for youngsters. The pretty cotton throw rug provides a counterpoint to the rich-looking hardwood—as well as a soft place to sit.

Cork. Also used on walls and ceilings, cork tiles are made from the granulated bark of the cork oak tree. Naturally sound-insulating, they're sold in various thicknesses, densities, and finishes—plain, waxed, polyurethane-sealed, and vinyl-bonded. You can get vinylized cork with veined patterns, stripes, and other designs.

An active youngster can give a cork floor a beating, so choose tiles with a hard protective finish. Expect to pay about $5 to $8 per square foot.

Wood Floors

A wood floor adds warmth and beauty to a room. But it doesn't absorb sound well and isn't very comfortable to sit on, although adding a rug or two can alleviate both problems.

Most wood flooring comes in narrow strips of random lengths, or in planks of various widths and random lengths. It's milled in several thicknesses and comes in two forms: tongue and groove, which creates a strong interlocking joint, and square-edge, which is nailed through the top. You can also get wood tiles.

Wood flooring may be factory-finished or left unfinished, to be sanded and finished in place. A new wood floor, installed, costs about $7.50 to $15 per square foot, depending on wood type, quality, and finish.

An existing wood floor can be refinished to make it stain and water resistant; professionals usually charge from $2 to $5 per square foot.

Another option is to paint the floor. Your creativity is the only limit —you may decide on a solid color, use

DESIGN: SUNDAY HENDRICKSON

a geometric or freeform design, reproduce a hopscotch grid or other game pattern, or stencil on a design. Protect the paint with polyurethane or another sealer.

Wall-to-wall Carpet

Carpeting makes a nice soft surface for rough play and helps deaden sound, but it's not as practical as hard flooring for young kids. It's more difficult to keep clean, and it won't let blocks be stacked as easily or wheeled toys be rolled as smoothly as on a resilient or wood floor. One type of carpet is designed to promote activity—it comes imprinted with patterns for games such as hopscotch, Chinese checkers, or tick-tack-toe.

Wall-to-wall carpeting is more appropriate in an older child's room, but only you will know whether it's right for your child. You'll be throwing your money away unless your child treats the carpet with some respect.

Generally, man-made carpeting causes fewer allergies than do natural materials (see section on allergies on page 12). Because of its wearability, 100-percent nylon is a good choice. Spills wipe up more easily if the carpet is treated with a stain repellent. Most nylon carpets have a built-in static resistance. By law, all carpets are fire retardant.

A low-pile or short-loop, densely woven carpet is best if it's going into a nursery or toddler's room. A deep shag can conceal objects that a small child might swallow. Plush carpets also hold a lot of dust, which is unhealthy for infants to breathe. A medium color shows less dirt than a very light or dark color, and a variegated texture or pattern will camouflage stains.

Expect to pay from about $5 to $15 per square yard for carpeting a kid's room; remnants, commercial grades, and indoor-outdoor carpeting can save you money. Carpeting printed with game-board designs ranges from about $11 to $18 per square yard.

Rugs

Large area rugs or small throw rugs can be placed strategically on a resilient or wood floor to create soft, comfortable places to sit or play.

While forming cozy islands in a room, throw rugs still allow space for activities that need a flat surface. The most practical throw rugs have a nonslip backing and are machine washable. Throw rugs created for kids come in whimsical shapes and storybook designs. Fluffy bathroom mats, sold in a wide range of colors, are an inexpensive option.

Area rugs cover more territory than throw rugs, making them more expensive and harder to keep clean. Purely decorative rugs (ones designed as area rugs or wall-to-wall carpet remnants with the edges bound) may be more appropriate for older children, since they leave less smooth floor space for games. For young kids, you can opt for a game-board rug produced by a manufacturer who prints games on wall-to-wall carpeting (see at left).

Instead of just sitting on the floor, some rugs educate, entertain, or engage kids in activities. Clockwise from top left: a play rug with roadways along which kids can wheel little wooden cars; a sports-theme rug designed to spark a young one's imagination; and a hopscotch board that comes with beanbag markers. All are fire resistant and have nonskid backing.

WALL TREATMENTS

The ideal wall treatment in a kid's room is not only pleasing to the eye, but also durable and easy to clean. Some treatments serve additional functions—for example, a bulletin board can keep your child organized, and a chalkboard can encourage creativity.

Paint

Painting is one of the simplest, most economical ways to decorate a room. Repaint every few years for a fresh look or to keep pace with your child's changing color preferences. You can change the whole look of the space by investing as little as $10 in painting the trim, or spend several hundred dollars on a mural.

Latex paint has a water base, making it practically odorless, easy to apply, and fast-drying—and tools wash up quickly with soap and water. A flat or eggshell finish is the usual choice for walls and ceilings. For trim and areas that get heavy wear, choose a semigloss enamel. Glossy finishes are more washable and durable, but any nick or bump is highlighted by their sheen.

You can select a single color or use several to complement the furnishings. Or you can choose something fancier: murals and stenciling are decorative paint techniques that work especially well in children's rooms.

Fuchsia Zs and black and blue stars stenciled on the wall over the bed are designed to lull the occupant of this room to sleep. The bedding picks up the colors of the stencils as well as of the golden backdrop.

If you don't want to tackle an elaborate finish yourself and don't have the budget for a professional, try something simple and playful. For example, you could dip your hands into paint and cover the wall with palm prints.

Chalkboards

Almost any smooth surface can be transformed into a chalkboard by covering it with special chalkboard paint, available at most paint stores. The paint is a flat alkyd that comes in green or black.

Apply it directly to the wall, or coat a piece of hardboard that you attach to the wall. Use two or three coats; and if the surface to be painted is wood, seal it with a primer first.

The chalkboard can be a simple rectangle or a more elaborate shape—for example, an animal silhouette. Consider placing a strip of concave picture molding at the lower edge of the board to hold the chalk and eraser and to catch chalk dust.

Wallpaper

You'll find choosing is easier if you bring along paint chips, samples of upholstery fabrics, and other colors and patterns you plan to use. Also have with you a diagram of the room with the dimensions clearly marked (and with placement and sizes of doors and windows shown) so the sales staff can calculate how much wallpaper you need to buy.

The back of a wallpaper sample usually contains information on the wallpaper's content and says whether or not the material is prepasted, washable, or able to be stripped easily.

Vinyl coverings are practical in a child's room. Fabric-backed vinyl and scrubbable solid vinyl are most durable and easy to clean (even crayon marks come off); expect to pay around $15 to $30 a roll. Vinyl-coated and expanded-vinyl products, costing $8 to $15 a roll, aren't as cleanable. If the walls are bumpy or poorly finished, choose a wallpaper with a textured finish to hide the imperfections.

Abstract patterns, especially ones with bold colors, are usually better choices for kids' rooms than juvenile themes that will soon be outgrown. If you can't deny your child a faddish design he or she craves, put it on a single wall so that replacing it later won't require too much effort or money.

Ask for patterns that come with matching fabrics and bedding if you want a coordinated look. Also make sure that pictures and other wall-mounted items will work with the wallpaper pattern.

A border—used alone or to complement a wallpaper—is a relatively inexpensive way to jazz up a child's room. Since borders can be changed easily, you can indulge a young child in a juvenile motif—such as dinosaurs, cowboys, trains, or letters of the alphabet—without committing the room permanently to the look.

Borders don't have to go at the top of the wall—they can be applied lower down, where youngsters can see them without craning their necks. A chair-rail border divides the room horizontally: you could paint the walls different colors or use different wallpaper patterns above and below the border, or you could wallpaper one part and paint the other. Some borders look effective placed just above the baseboard, giving toddlers a close-up view of the design. Another option is to use a border around doors and windows.

Paneling

Solid boards or sheet paneling add a decorative touch while protecting the walls. For example, paneling 3 or 4 feet high near the bed defines the sleeping area and guards against soil marks.

The most expensive choice, solid boards are pieces of lumber milled to overlap or interlock. Boards come in a wide range of widths, thicknesses, and lengths. To keep costs down, choose materials stocked locally.

The main types of sheet paneling are plywood and hardboard, both commonly sold in 4- by 8-foot pieces. Plywood consists of thin layers of wood peeled from lumber and glued together; hardboard is made from wood fibers bonded under pressure.

You can get just about any kind of wood laminated to plywood panels. Hardboard paneling comes with imitation wood finishes, or it can be embossed with a pattern. Plywood is more expensive than hardboard, but it's also more durable and less subject to warping and moisture damage.

Sold rolled up like a poster, this specially coated sheet of paper works just like a chalkboard (above). After being purchased, it was cut into the shape of a whale to suit its young owner.

A stars-and-stripes wallpaper border (right) applied to the window recess frames the arch and carries through the patriotic theme.

Bulletin Boards

You can buy a ready-made bulletin board to hang on the wall, or you can make your own by covering an entire wall with cork or fabric-wrapped fiberboard.

Cork is sold in tiles at some floor-covering stores and in sheets at home-improvement centers. Sheet cork, sold by the linear foot from rolls, is much less expensive than tiles. You can get a linear foot of 4-foot-wide cork (equivalent to four tiles) for not much more than you'd pay for one or two tiles. Sheet goods come in up to ¼-inch thickness, while the most substantial tiles are only ⅛ inch thick.

If you don't want pinholes in the wall underneath the cork, glue the cork to soft fiberboard panels (available in 4- by 8-foot rectangles) and screw the panels to wall studs.

You can skip the cork altogether, and use fabric-wrapped fiberboard as a bulletin-board surface. Any coarse fabric that is strong and won't easily ravel will do. Burlap is a practical choice, since its weave will hide the pinholes.

Decorative Moldings

Wood moldings are an inexpensive way to add character to a room. They come in many standard patterns and sizes. You can get them natural, prefinished (painted or stained), or wrapped in vinyl. You can also buy plastic, vinyl, and aluminum moldings that look like wood. Molding systems come with corner pieces that eliminate the need for tricky cuts and joints.

One way to use molding is to divide a wall horizontally. Paint or wallpaper the sections differently for extra interest. You can also put hooks on a chair-rail molding or hang pictures from it.

Other Wall Decor

Pictures are a popular decoration in kids' rooms, just as in other areas of

Denim makes a handsome bulletin board surface in this Western-theme room (top). A cushiony wall hanging (bottom) adds three-dimensional interest to a nursery or toddler's room.

the house. Hang them framed or, if you can tolerate a more casual approach, let your child tack up posters of favorite sports heroes, rock stars, or other celebrities.

For young kids, try the colorful, cushiony wall hangings sold at many children's stores. Priced from about $20 to $80, they come in the shape of airplanes, clouds, balloons, and many other objects.

Borders and decals that are repositionable are another good choice for younger children. Kids' stores and catalogs sell room-decorating kits (about $25 to about $55) containing a continuous border and precut, peel-off appliqués. Designs include dinosaur, circus, football, and undersea motifs that even very young kids can stick on the wall and rearrange by themselves.

WINDOW TREATMENTS

A cute or cleverly designed window covering will quickly lose its charm unless it's sturdy, easy to clean, and simple for your child to operate. It should also control light the way you intend. A room-darkening treatment can help a small child who takes daytime naps settle down more easily.

The most common window coverings are curtains, blinds, shades, and shutters. There's no need to restrict yourself to a single treatment; you can combine two or more.

Curtains

Choose ready-to-hang or custom curtains, or make them yourself. Specialty bedding shops and catalogs offer ready-made curtains as a standard element in many of their coordinated bed-linen sets. For a custom job, look for fabrics designed especially for kids' rooms—many of them come with matching wallpaper.

Washable, medium-weight cotton and cotton-polyester blends are the most practical curtain fabrics for kids' rooms. Fabric of 100-percent cotton holds bright colors particularly well, although it will fade and rot in the sun unless the curtains are lined. Polyester blended with cotton makes the fabric more lightfast, rot resistant, and wrinkle-proof.

Curtains should be lined with a blackout material if you want the room dark in early morning and on summer evenings. Sheer curtains are fine if you use them in conjunction with a light-blocking shade or blind.

If your child is very young, do yourself a favor by ending the curtains at the bottom of the window frame. Little kids like to tug on floor-length treatments or hide behind them.

Blinds

Available with metal, vinyl, or wood slats, blinds offer the best way to control light. Lowering the blind and closing the slats dims the room, opening the slats lets in some light, and raising the blind floods the room with light.

Stock blinds are fine if you can get ones that fit the window opening exactly. Otherwise, get made-to-measure blinds, especially for an inside mount. Even at custom prices, most blinds are economical. Don't get the most expensive ones for a kid's room, though—the slats are bound to be dented or broken, and the operating mechanism may prove to be an irresistible toy.

Miniblinds with 1-inch metal or vinyl slats are the most common type of blind sold. You can get them in solid colors or in several colors to form horizontal stripes. Vinyl minis are appealing for kids' rooms because they're much less expensive than

Bows and flounces fill this little girl's room. Adding to the feminine appeal are ruffled valances over light-filtering dotted-swiss sheer curtains. Using the same fabric for valances, bedding, and upholstery establishes a coordinated look.

metal ones—although they're flimsier, come in fewer colors, don't close as tightly, and can warp in a hot spot.

Wood blinds, especially ones with wide slats, are often used as a substitute for shutters. Although twice as expensive as good-quality mini-blinds, they're about half the price of custom shutters. Because of their cost, you want to feel fairly confident that your child won't mistreat them. Their weight may make them too heavy for a young child to use.

Shades

The many styles include roller, pleated, Roman, and balloon shades. They range from sheer to opaque, so make sure the shade will control light the way you want. Also keep in mind that most shades allow little ventilation once they're lowered. Costs vary widely, depending on design, materials, workmanship, and the operating mechanism.

Roller shades are a good choice for kids' rooms—although some youngsters find them fascinating playthings. You can trim costs but still get a custom product by sewing or gluing a design onto an inexpensive ready-made shade. Another option is to embellish the shade with fabric paints matching the room's decor.

Shutters

You can adjust shutters to let in a little or a lot of light. They can also cut drafts when closed.

Custom shutters are an investment that will still be there when your child is in college and you've turned the room into a den or spare bedroom. Expect to pay several hundred dollars for a top-quality shutter to fit a standard double-hung window.

For a small fraction of the price, you can get stock shutters from a home-improvement center or lumber yard—but they may not last as long, especially if your child is particularly rough on furnishings.

This window shade (top) serves a dual purpose when it's pulled down: darkening the room and teaching arithmetic. Such a design can be stenciled onto a plain, ready-made shade with acrylic paints. Miniblinds framed by an envelope curtain (bottom) allow great flexibility in controlling light.

LIGHTING

Good lighting results when you use the appropriate fixture and light source (bulb or tube) for the situation. Keep in mind that safety is the key consideration when choosing lighting for young children. Fixtures that are out of reach or won't easily tip over are the best. Those within reach should contain a low-wattage light source that won't burn curious fingers. Other safety features include covers or caps on unused electrical outlets and wire reels to store excess lamp cord.

LIGHTING FIXTURES

You'll find plenty of fixtures to fit most budgets at lighting stores and home-improvement centers, as well as through decorators and lighting designers. But the choice of fixtures with juvenile themes is limited, even at stores catering to kids. If you can't find exactly what you want, consult local electrical supply stores. Many such shops will build fixtures from toys or other items that you provide.

Here are the types of fixtures most commonly used in kids' rooms.

Ceiling Fixtures

A single overhead fixture is usually the main source of general lighting in a child's room. For very young children, an overhead light makes the

Fixtures with kid appeal include these table lamps, clip-ons, floor lamps, and night-lights. The coat-rack lamp not only provides light but also shoe storage and a place to hang clothes.

room less scary and provides enough illumination for play. It's also the safest, since kids can't knock it over or burn themselves. Putting the fixture on a dimmer helps regulate the amount of light in the room.

Track fixtures are widely used to light specific task areas. They make it easy to redirect light to keep pace with a child's changing needs.

Wall Fixtures

Lighting designers who favor wall fixtures in children's rooms say that kids can't tip them over. Those dead-set against the fixtures say that kids sometimes like to hang from them. You'll have to be the one to decide if such a fixture is appropriate in your situation.

To provide general lighting, a wall fixture should be positioned high enough to bounce light off the ceiling. If the room isn't hard-wired for a wall fixture, you can surface-mount the fixture and plug it into an electrical outlet. Try to hide the cord behind heavy furniture such as a dresser, bookcase, or bed.

Table Lamps

These are the fixtures most commonly available with juvenile themes. Usually the motif is restricted to the base, which may appear in the shape of a crayon, boat, airplane, or storybook character. Other types have plain bases and brightly colored or patterned shades. Others sold for the nursery have built-in baby monitors or music boxes.

Of course, a table lamp doesn't have to have an upright base and removable shade. It can be a gooseneck or other type with a movable arm that allows your child to adjust the light to the proper height.

A table lamp should be weighted so that it doesn't tip over easily. For added safety, you can screw the base to the furniture, just as hotels do. Reduce danger further by buying a wire reel to store excess lamp cord.

A bedside lamp should have an on/off switch that your child can easily reach and operate. Avoid "touch lamps," which turn on or off when lightly tapped. They're easily knocked over at night, and young children can frighten themselves by accidentally operating the lamp.

Floor Lamps

These sometimes look like play equipment to a toddler and can tip over easily, so reserve them for older ages.

The many floor styles include jointed types that allow you to move the light closer for reading or other activities; pole lamps containing several lights; and torchères, which bounce light off the ceiling to provide general illumination without glare.

Clip-on Lights

These fixtures, which come in both swivel and gooseneck styles, can go where table lamps don't fit—such as on a headboard or attached to the top bunk of a bunk bed. They're space savers on a crowded desk. Clip-ons can also be clamped to shelves to focus light on collections. Test the fixture before buying to make sure it fastens securely to a surface.

Night-lights

Some types plug into an electrical outlet and automatically glow when the room is dark. Others have tiny bulbs and have to be switched on. You'll even find types that attach to cribs.

Juvenile themes are common. For example, you can get night-lights in the shape of cartoon characters or large glowing crayons.

LIGHT SOURCES

The quality and intensity of light depend on the type of bulb or tube you use. Some fixtures are manufactured to accept a certain type.

Keep in mind that using the proper wattage is essential to protect your child's eyes. Too much light is as bad as too little. You may have to experiment to find the right level for different tasks.

Incandescent

Most widely used in homes, incandescent light is produced by a tungsten thread burning slowly inside a glass bulb. Since the majority of wavelengths are in the red and yellow portion of the color spectrum, incandescent light has a warm quality. On the minus side, incandescent light creates glare and shadows, and is the least energy-efficient light source.

Fluorescent

Produced when electricity causes the phosphor coating inside a tube to glow, fluorescent light is unrivaled for energy efficiency. It also minimizes glare and shadows. Manufacturers have now developed fluorescents in a wide spectrum of colors, so there's no longer any need to put up with a harsh bluish or greenish quality.

In addition to the standard long tubes, you can now buy U-shaped compact tubes, which can replace incandescent bulbs in some fixtures. Miniature tubes in round and cylindrical shapes fit standard lamps.

Halogen

These small, long-lasting bulbs operate much like incandescent bulbs, except that halogen gas surrounding the filament produces an intensely bright light. The bulbs are used in special fixtures with built-in transformers.

Because of their extreme heat, halogens aren't recommended for areas where youngsters can get at them and possibly be burned. Also, touching a bulb with a finger leaves oil on it, which damages the surface and can cause the bulb to explode.

INDEX

Boldface numbers refer to photographs.